Reinaldo Domingos

Money Boy
Friends helping friends

1st Edition

About the series

The series "Money Boy" is a children's adaptation based upon the DSOP Financial Education Methodology, conceived by master, professor, educator, and financial therapist Reinaldo Domingos.

The series is part of the DSOP Financial Education Program that ranges from grammar school to college. It consists of 30 didactic volumes (15 textbooks and 15 teacher's books) and six paradidactic volumes that comprise subjects of family, diversity, sustainability, autonomy, and citizenship.

In addition to the books, the schools that adopt the DSOP Financial Education Program are entitled to pedagogical training, financial education workshops for teachers, lectures for the students and the community, and access to the school website (portalescolas.dsop.com.br), which consists of class plans, interactive activities (games), videos, and exclusive access to students, teachers, parents, and school managers.

For further information, please visit www.dsop.com.br/escolas or contact a local franchisee in your area by searching on our website www.dsop.com.br/franquia.

What's happening

In this third book of the series, Money Boy and his friends get together to tackle new challenges. Another year has begun in Lagoa Branca town. At Money Boy's home, family values are renewed with the arrival of another family member.

He joins his old friend Spender at school and meets Victoria, a girl with brown hair and dimples on her cheeks. The three of them get together to tackle life challenges.

Spender has an unsolvable problem that makes him sad. Victoria needs to recover from a small accident. Money Boy decides to make up a master plan to help them all.

In the classroom teacher Raymoney's lessons teach them to put ideas into practice and change them into entrepreneurship projects. Money Boy sticks to the goal of spreading the **DSOP Methodology** to all. Victoria tries to teach her mother that magic formula which can transform the financial health of her home.

Spender finds out that there are dreams that cannot be purchased, no matter how wealthy you are. Together, the three of them join forces and share their dreams.

©Editora DSOP, 2016
©Reinaldo Domingos, 2015

President
Reinaldo Domingos

Text editor
Andrei Sant'Anna
Renata de Sá

Art editor
Denise Patti Vitiello
Christine Baptista

Illustrator
Ariel Fajtlowicz

Editorial producer
Amanda Torres

English language version
Joan Rumph
Milena Cavichiolo

All rights reserved to Editora DSOP
Av. Paulista, 726 - Cj. 1210 - Bela Vista
ZIP Code: 01310-910 - Brazil - São Paulo - SP
Phone: 55 11 3177-7800
www.editoradsop.com.br

```
       Dados Internacionais de Catalogação na Publicação (CIP)
                (Câmara Brasileira do Livro, SP, Brasil)

     Domingos, Reinaldo
        Money boy : friends helping friends / Reinaldo
     Domingos ; illustration Ariel Fajtlowicz ;
     translation Joan Rumph e Milena Cavichiolo. --
     São Paulo : Editora DSOP, 2015.

        Título original: O menino do dinheiro : ação
     entre amigos
        ISBN 978-85-8276-115-1

        1. Dinheiro - Literatura infantojuvenil
     2. Finanças - Literatura infantojuvenil
     I. Fajtlowicz, Ariel. II. Título.


     14-11830                                      CDD-028.5
```

Índices para catálogo sistemático:

1. Educação financeira : Literatura infantil
   028.5
2. Educação financeira : Literatura infantojuvenil
   028.5

Contents

Great news 7

Who are we? 15

Good ideas 21

A problem without a solution 27

A place in the world 31

A masterplan 35

The magic formula 41

The secret mission 47

Word of honor 51

Magic mirror on the wall 55

Giving up is for the weak 61

Roll call 67

The best things in the world 73

Tears of joy 77

Special in a different way 81

Great news

In the small town of Lagoa Branca, the children enjoyed the last few days of their school vacation while their parents hurried off to work.

Money Boy, always with a smile on his face, rode his new bike around the neighborhood. He was anxious for the start of the new school year. He missed the math lessons of Mr. Raymoney, the tricks of his friend Spender and the art classes taught by Mrs. Constance. His school uniform and backpack were ready.

Money Boy knew that, within a few days, he would be back in class, leaning new things, meeting new teachers, and joining his old friends. He couldn't wait to tell everyone the great news!

Money Boy's heart pumped fast, as he thought about all the good things that had happened recently. He learned to save his coins and take care of his piggy banks; he met Mr. Raymoney, who told him about the **DSOP Methodology**; he began to receive a monthly allowance; and he taught his father how to save some of the money he earned. In addition, Money Boy was thrilled with the new bike he received for his birthday. Lastly, he received exciting news that would change his life forever.

The week went by quickly and finally the long-awaited school day came. On that rainy afternoon, while walking through the school corridors, Money Boy spotted Spender. He also seemed lost in the confusion of new students and classes on the first day of school.

"Spender! So good to see you! How was your vacation?"

"I travelled with my dad. We spent a few days on the beach and I learned how to surf! It was really cool! How about you?"

"I stayed at home. Took time to enjoy my new bike and learned how to jump over obstacles with it."

"Cool! I want to learn that, too."

"Sure! And I have great news to tell you," Money Boy began to say.

Suddenly, Mrs. Constance interrupted the conversation, telling the kids to enter the second room to the left, where Ms. Help was about to begin her class.

The two of them marched off to their room. Money Boy was anxious to tell the good news to his friend, who had become very curious. Still, they would have to wait until the end of class to talk.

Ms. Help welcomed the new class.

"Good afternoon everyone! Welcome back to school! For those who don't know me yet, my name is Ms. Help. This year I'll be teaching you English and Writing."

Money Boy - Friends helping friends

"Please take out your notebooks, because our first writing assignment is about to begin," Ms. Help said, wasting no time.

"I'd like you to write a three-paragraph composition on the subject of, 'Who Am I?' This way I'll get to know you better. Let's go now. Let's start writing!"

Money Boy scratched his head and thought three paragraphs were too short for the many things he wanted to tell his new teacher. He glanced at the girl in the row next to him with the brown, curly hair. She had a couple of small dimples on her cheeks when she smiled.

The girl slowly raised her hand, "Ms. Help, what if we still don't know who we are? What should we do to complete these three paragraphs?"

"What's your name, dear?" the teacher asked.

"My name is Victoria." the girl replied.

"Victoria, it's not that complicated. Tell me about your dreams, things you like to do to have fun."

The class finally became silent and Money Boy began to write.

Dear Teacher,

My name is Ray.

Since I was a small kid, I enjoyed playing in the backyard, having fun and buying candy and ice cream near my house.

People used to call me Little Ray.

When I turned four, my mother gave me a piggy bank and I started to put coins inside it. I learned that if I spent less money on candy and ice cream, and saved coins throughout the year, I could make a dream come true. After realizing that, I started filling up more piggy banks and achieved even bigger dreams. That's how I became known as Money Boy.

Last year, I met a teacher who has the same name as mine — Ray. His nickname is Raymoney, and he taught me a magical formula that helps people to organize their finances in order to achieve their dreams. It's a methodology called DSOP, which in Portuguese means Diagnosing, Dreaming, Budgeting and Saving. These four little words have changed the life of my family. I tell everyone this secret, so more people can make their dreams come true as well.

My mother often said I was a determined child and wouldn't give up until I got what I wanted. I think she was absolutely right!

Money Boy looked around and saw his classmates with their heads down writing in their notebooks. Everybody focused on the assignment except Victoria, who was deep in thought and hadn't written a line of her composition yet.

At the end of class, Ms. Help told the students they would receive textbooks to use throughout the year.

"Take good care of them, so they can be returned at the end of the school year and other students can use them in the future," she instructed. "If you lose or damage your book, you will have to pay for it."

The students handed in their assignment, grabbed a book, and left the classroom. Victoria walked to the front of the room with her eyes looking down, feeling upset that she hadn't been able to finish her writing assignment. Ms. Help noticed the girl's paperwork as she laid it on top of the pile of compositions.

"Victoria, would you like to finish your assignment at home and turn it in tomorrow?" Ms. Help asked. Victoria looked up and with a deep sigh of relief, she nodded YES!

When the bell rang, everybody met outside in the courtyard. It was the best time of the day—break time. Money Boy walked over to Spender to resume their conversation and to tell him his great news. As they began to talk, a loud noise followed by a commotion, broke up their meeting once again. They ran outside to see what had happened and saw their new classmate lying down on the ground.

Victoria didn't see the puddle next to the trees. She had slipped and fallen. Some kids were standing around laughing, while others attempted to pick up her books. Spender and Money Boy helped her up and tried to clean her stuff off. Water dripped from Victoria's uniform and her books looked like they had been soaked in mud. The girl's new notebook was completely ruined, along with her textbook. Victoria started to remember the warning Ms. Help had given to the students about their books.

Money Boy - Friends helping friends

The dimples on her cheeks had vanished and a steady stream of tears ran down her face. She knew her parents couldn´t afford to buy new school supplies so soon. Devastated, she told her two new friends that her family was going through a very difficult time.

Money Boy spoke up and promised Victoria that he would help solve her problem. He didn't know how to do it yet, but he asked her to trust him. Money Boy would do anything to see those two dimples reappear on Victoria's cheeks.

Who are we?

On her way back home, Victoria tried to figure out how to tell her mother what had happened. The girl kept asking herself why her day had turned out to be so bad. She had been so excited to go to school, and in the end, everything had gone wrong.

Mrs. Efficiency, Victoria's mother, was at home working at her sewing machine when her daughter walked in the door looking sad. "How was your first day at school, honey?"

"Oh, mom, you don't want to know!" the girl cried.

"What happened, dear? Come over here, sit down, and tell me what happened." Mrs. Efficiency pulled over a chair so Victoria could sit beside her.

"For starters, I don't know who I am!" said the girl with an anxious expression on her face.

"What do you mean?" the mother asked.

"Today, Ms. Help gave us an assignment to write a composition called, 'Who Am I?' In my class, everybody wrote three paragraphs except me. Is it possible that all my classmates are able to tell who they are and I can't?"

"Oh, my dear, that's not a very easy task. It's okay to find it difficult. We discover who we are gradually. With new life experiences, we learn and change ourselves a little every day," said the mother, trying to comfort her daughter.

"And how can we find that out, mom?"

"Life always presents us with challenges, and the way each one of us faces them is what defines who we are," Mrs. Efficiency explained.

Victoria was still sad and deep in thought. Her mother wanted to know why she was feeling like that, and then she handed her the textbook and the notebook, both still wet and dirty. "Victoria, what happened to your school books?"

"Well, mom, I took them with me on my school break. The courtyard was wet and I slipped and fell on the ground. Everybody was laughing at me. It was an awful day. I should have stayed in bed."

"Don't say that, honey. Getting up from bed each day and facing the challenges of life is a blessing, though, at times, things can seem harsh. Remember what I told you about challenges?"

Money Boy - Friends helping friends

"I do" the girl answered in a meek voice.

"So that's it. Children also have their challenges to face. Those were challenges life put in front of you today. The way you reacted to them reveals slightly who you are," Mrs. Efficiency said.

"And how am I supposed to react to those problems, mom?" Victoria asked, looking confused.

"I don't know, dear, but believe me, the answer is there. Go wash up before dinner. Afterwards we'll get together and talk about it more."

Victoria thought some more about what her mother had said. Life was challenging and she wanted to face her problems and feel strong, but she still felt unhappy.

In her room she spent a while looking at herself in the mirror.

"Who am I?" she asked the mirror.

In her mind, she was a girl without books and without answers to her questions.

At home, Money Boy was deep in thought, too. He had promised his new classmate that he would help her. After dinner, he talked to his mother and came up with an idea.

"Mom, I want to crack open my piggy bank," he announced.

"Why is that honey? It isn't full yet."

"Well, I know I should open it only when it is full, but I have a good reason to break that rule."

Money Boy told Mrs. Foresight the difficulties his classmate, Victoria, was going through and said the coins in his piggy bank might be enough to buy a new book for the girl.

"Son, in that case, it really is an emergency. You are right," said his mother, showing her support. "One of the reasons we save money is so we can use it in time of need. We should help people in need, too. I'm proud of you for being so generous."

"Tomorrow, before going to school, I'll stop by the bookstore to buy another book for Victoria," Money Boy said.

The mother nodded and the boy was about to leave the room but turned to ask her another question.

"Victoria has a couple of small holes in her cheeks that only appear when she smiles. Is that normal?" he asked.

"Yes, son. They are called dimples."

"Dimples?" repeated the boy.

"Yes. They are small holes that appear on the cheek or chin when someone smiles. Not everyone has them though," Mrs. Foresight explained to her curious son.

"Only on someone that is special?" Money Boy wanted to know.

"Do you think Victoria is a special girl?" his mother asked.

"I do," he answered.

"She must be special then!" Mrs. Foresight said with a grin.

Money Boy - Friends helping friends

The boy went to his room as happy as ever. His mother had approved his decision of opening the piggy bank. In an emergency, having money saved was helpful to solving some problems. He felt he was doing the right thing. Besides helping his friend, he would be able to see her beautiful dimples when she smiled again.

Good ideas

The next morning, Money Boy came to school anxious to meet Victoria. He wanted to give her the brand new book he had purchased with the coins from his piggy bank.

Unexpectedly, his friend Spender approached him.

"Aren't you going to tell me the great news after all? I was curious yesterday and you walked away and didn't tell me anything."

"That's right. Spender, you're not going to believe it. I'm so happy!" Money Boy began with a look of excitement.

At that moment, both of them saw Victoria and waved for her to come closer.

"Victoria, I have a little something for you. Remember I promised to help you?" Money Boy asked.

"I do remember. It's just that I have thought about that so much since yesterday, it makes my head hurt," Victoria admitted.

"Look, I had a piggy bank that I saved a few coins in. Yesterday, I cracked it open, took the money out, and used it to buy you a new book," said the boy handing over the gift to Victoria.

"Wow, I don't believe it! I can't thank you enough!" Victoria cried.

"Ah, you can smile and that's plenty!" Money Boy answered.

"Listen, as soon as I can, I promise to give you the money back so you can fill up a new piggy bank," the girl said.

"You don't have to. It's a gift from me to you," Money Boy added. "Just pretend it's your birthday present ahead of time."

Spender interrupted because he could not hold back his curiosity any longer. "So, are you going to tell me your great news or not?" he pleaded.

Victoria spoke up, "What great news?"

"Oh boy, I've got to tell you, I am the happiest boy in the world! Last week I found out something that is going to change my life forever. It is something no money in the world can buy."

"What is so wonderful then?" Spender asked.

"I'm going to have a little brother!" Money Boy announced.

"Wow, that's great, congratulations!" Victoria said.

"Yeah! I'm anxious for him to arrive as soon as possible. I'm going to teach him how to play baseball, ride a bike, collect toy cars, have piggy banks, save money, and lots of other things. Everything I know, about every possible subject in the world, I'm going to teach my little brother," Money Boy said with confidence.

"Your eyes shine when you talk," said Victoria. "They look like two small, bright lights."

"I have bright lights and you have little dimples!" Money Boy said, smiling.

It was then that they both noticed Spender didn't seem to enjoy hearing the news. On the contrary, he looked sad.

"Spender, what's up man? Why are you sad? Didn't you like hearing that my little brother is on his way?" Money Boy asked.

"Ah, it's not that. I'm happy for you. It's just that today I have a toothache, but the pain will go away soon. Let's go to class," Spender replied, trying to change the subject.

"I'm still without a notebook. Could you please lend me some sheets of paper out of yours?" Victoria asked.

"Of course! We can think about getting you another notebook," said Money Boy, still suspicious about the way Spender had reacted to his good news.

The three of them entered the classroom and Mr. Raymoney was already writing notes on the board.

"Well class, our math project this year is going to be about entrepreneurship," the teacher began.

"Entrepr... what?" Spender asked.

"Entrepreneurship," Mr. Raymoney repeated.

"And what's that?" Victoria asked.

"Putting an idea into practice," the teacher said. "It's about having a plan and making it happen."

"Is it the same as working?" Money Boy asked.

"Yes, that too. It's having an idea, putting it into practice, and then obtaining the results."

The students were silent and a little confused. Then the teacher decided to give an example, because that way it would be easier for the class to understand what entrepreneurship is all about.

"When I was a kid, my father decided he would grow tomatoes in the backyard of our house, so my mother could save some money at the market," Mr. Raymoney started to explain.

"He did some research, followed the instructions for planting tomatoes, and learned many new things. For instance, if tomatoes are overwatered they will begin to split. After a while, my father realized that growing tomatoes proved to be a good idea. Every week we had more tomatoes than we could eat. He then asked two friends to help him plant and cultivate the soil, and they started producing many more tomatoes," Mr. Raymoney said.

"My father started to sell those tomatoes to his neighbors. Later, he began growing other vegetables. We became better off and managed to remodel our house and travel on vacation. Everything became better for us in the family," the teacher concluded.

"So that's what entrepreneurship is all about?" Victoria asked.

"Yes, Victoria. My father had the idea of growing tomatoes. He learned from books how to do it and began growing them in our backyard. The purpose was to have enough for us to eat. He was an entrepreneur as well," Mr. Raymoney explained.

"Now it's clearer, Mr. Raymoney. My father is also an entrepreneur," said Spender.

"Is that so? What does he do?" the teacher asked.

"He had the idea of creating a new fruit-based soda pop. He did some tests and had good results. In the beginning, he would sell a few bottles with the help of my uncles. Then the beverage became popular in the neighborhood and soon everyone in the city started drinking the soda my father invented. Next, he created the brand "Cool Stuff." Today, the company sells sodas and ice cream all over the country," Spender stated proudly

"That' a wonderful example of entrepreneurship, Spender." Mr. Raymoney said.

The students were sitting up, waiting to hear more when the bell rang for their break. Before the students left, Mr. Raymoney mentioned that in the next class they would learn entrepreneurship lessons in seven steps.

The students gathered outside in the schoolyard and talked about all they had learned in their last class. Everyone seemed to be bitten by the "entrepreneurship bug."

However, Victoria, Money Boy and Spender were not thinking about that. They had a problem to solve. Victoria's notebook had been soaked in water and she couldn't take notes anymore.

"Let's think together," said Money Boy.

"You know, I was taking notes about entrepreneurship on the paper I borrowed from you and remembered that my father works in a paper factory," Victoria said. "I have an idea, but I don't know if it's going to work."

"What idea?" Spender asked.

"I think I could ask my dad if there is any leftover paper at the factory. I could grab a bunch of paper and staple them together to form a notebook," Victoria replied.

"Great idea! We can help you with that. We can draw on the cover to make your notebook more beautiful!" said Money Boy, trying to help his friend.

"We can glue some pictures on it, too," added Victoria.

The three of them were there for a while planning how they could make a new notebook for the girl. Then they went to the cafeteria to buy something to eat and made a toast with grape juice.

"Here's to great ideas!" they all said at the same time.

A problem without a solution

At Victoria's house, something big was going on. It was Saturday and Money Boy and Spender were helping Victoria make her new notebook. Her father had brought home so many sheets of paper from the factory that they could make notebooks for everybody at school, if needed.

Scissors, crayons, glue, stapler, and string were scattered all over the floor. The girl's room was a big mess when her mother entered with a tray of snacks. While they were eating, Mrs. Efficiency carefully looked over the notebook covers they had made.

"Kids, I have an idea that might be cool!" she said.

"What idea, mom?" Victoria asked.

"I have some extra fabric downstairs that I can glue to cardboard and you can use it as a notebook cover."

And so, a handmade notebook was created with a new cover design. Victoria chose a plaid fabric of blue and white. She smiled proudly at her creation, showing off the two dimples on her cheeks.

Money Boy saw her smile and had even greater respect for her determination.

On Monday, Victoria came to school and became an instant attraction to her classmates. Everyone wanted to see the customized notebook. It was unique and there was nothing like it in the stores.

When the last class finished, several students came to Victoria and asked if her mother would make other notebooks like it, because they would love to have one. The girl said she would talk to her mother and give them a reply the next day.

On their way home, the three friends celebrated the success of the homemade notebook. They were especially excited for having made it with their own hands, along with the help of Mrs. Efficiency.

"I can't believe there was a happy solution to my problem!" Victoria shouted with joy.

"Last week I was sad and hopeless and now I'm here celebrating. Thanks for your help guys. I couldn't have done it without you!"

"Now we're all happy. You have your new book, your notebook, and I'm getting a new brother! Everything is working out perfect for us," Money Boy said cheerfully.

At that moment, Victoria and Money Boy noticed Spender had remained silent. He had turned his eyes away from his friends and a serious look appeared on his face.

"Spender, what's the matter? Talk to us. Maybe we can help," Money Boy insisted.

"Yeah! We're friends, we're here for you!" Victoria added. "Just like we managed to solve the issue with my book and notebook together, we can face any other problem."

"You know what? I'm really happy for you, but in my case, no one can help me. I have a problem without a solution," Spender replied.

"What do you mean a problem without a solution?" Victoria asked.

"A problem without a solution is a problem without a solution," Spender repeated.

"Are you sure about that?" asked Money Boy.

"I am," Spender whispered.

"Come on, speak up. If there isn't a solution at least you'll get it off your chest," said Victoria, poking him.

"Well, my problem can't be solved with money the way Money Boy did when he purchased you a new book, Victoria. Nor can it be solved with recycled material and creativity like what we did with your notebook. My problem is that I will never have what Money Boy is getting within a few months."

The three were silent for a few minutes.

"A little brother?" said the girl at last.

"Yes," Spender answered.

"But why is that?" Victoria wanted to know.

Money Boy cautiously said, "Because he doesn't have a mother."

"Gee, that's a complicated problem that one."

"What did I say? A problem without a solution," Spender muttered.

"A problem and no solution," Money Boy nodded in agreement.

"I've learned from my mother that life presents challenges to us and they happen so we can get to know ourselves better," Victoria said.

"A challenge?" asked Spender, interested in what the girl was trying to tell him.

"Yes! While I was down in the mud, with my school books all damaged, I also thought that was a problem without solution. Today, I'm here celebrating my experience and now I am a winner. I have learned to know myself better," she said.

"What are you trying to tell me?" asked Spender.

"That maybe life is posing you a challenge. You don't have a brother, but you wish to have one very much. That's your challenge and maybe you'll have to fight for it and win that challenge in the end," Victoria suggested.

"Yes, maybe," Spender hesitated. "But I don't know how to face that."

"We never know. Until we wake up someday with an idea in our head that might work out," Victoria added.

"If I could, I'd share my brother with you," said Money Boy. "Let's think about it together. For every problem, there is a solution. My mother always tells me that."

A place in the world

Upon arriving home, Victoria found her mother still working at her sewing machine. Excited, the girl decided to tell her about her day.

"Mom my new notebook was a big hit, you're not going to believe it!"

"That's great honey. Congratulations! I'm happy to have made a beautiful cover for you," said Mrs. Efficiency, dividing her attention between her sewing and Victoria.

Mr. Carreira, Victoria's father, was in the living room watching TV, when his daughter came in and sat down beside him on the couch.

"Honey, I'm so proud to see you growing up, learning things, and taking your place in the world," he said.

"Gee, dad, that' a beautiful thing to hear. "Taking my place in the world," repeated Victoria, imitating her father's rough voice.

Faced with so many compliments, Victoria believed it was an appropriate time to ask her mother to make new notebooks for her friends.

"Mom, Manuela and Claire said they would buy notebooks just like mine if you made them. What do you think of that? They'd be really happy, and we could choose other fabric prints from your leftover materials."

"Selling? Hmmm... I'm not sure if it's going to work," answered Mrs. Efficiency.

"And why is that mom? It's simple. You make some and I take them to school. Those who are willing to buy them will do so. And that way I'll be able to return Money Boy the amount that he paid for my new book."

Mrs. Efficiency found that a fair deal. She was grateful for what the boy had done and wanted to return the money to him. Victoria's mother then agreed to make some notebooks with the leftover paper from the factory where Mr. Carreira worked. She would also use fabric remains from her sewing that she would otherwise throw away.

Together, mother and daughter sorted out bags filled with pieces of fabric of all types, sizes, and textures to find what would be a pretty notebook cover.

Mr. Carreira saw both of them very focused on the job. "Victoria, mom is going to make the notebooks while you do your homework. Studying is your job; it's the most important thing for you to do now!"

"Ok, I know that. I'm going to do it now," the girl answered.

"That's right. Study hard so when you grow up, you'll guarantee your..."—the father started to say when the smart girl interrupted him.

"Place in the world!" Victoria finished his sentence, once again imitating her father's way of speaking.

A few weeks later, the girl with the dimples sold a bunch of notebooks, which became very popular at school. Victoria took notes of the orders in her notepad and gave them to her mother. A couple of days later, she delivered them to the students accordingly.

Things were working out fine, and Mrs. Efficiency was able to give her daughter a monthly allowance.

Happy as ever, the girl stood in front of the mirror in her room. She stared at her image for a while and then asked one more time, "Who am I?"

Countless thoughts raced through her head—thoughts of her having turned into a courageous girl, full of ideas, and willing to put them into practice.

"I am an entrepreneur!" she shouted.

"A young entrepreneur, looking for her place in the world! Victoria, I'm proud of you!" she laughed at herself, looking back at her reflection.

A masterplan

Money Boy and Spender were in the schoolyard talking about soccer when Victoria approached them.

"Hi there, I want to give you this, Money Boy," handing over to him an envelope.

Money Boy, being curious, opened it and saw some dollar bills inside.

"Victoria, what is all this money for?" he asked.

"Gee, Victoria, did you get all this by selling the notebooks?" interrupted Spender, impressed by the girl's craftiness.

"Yes," Victoria replied. "I mean the sales income goes to my mother, because it's her work. In fact, I'm getting a monthly allowance. I can now pay back Money Boy what he spent for the book he bought me in the beginning of the school year."

"Victoria, I told you, you don't owe me a thing," insisted Money Boy, giving the envelope back to the girl. "That was a gift."

She smiled and thanked him again, giving him a hug.

Victoria's creativity and her ability to get the word out quickly about the notebooks at school impressed Spender.

"Victoria, you sure have some talent. You'll end up becoming Money Girl," Spender said with a chuckle.

"It would be cool! But I think I still have a lot to learn from Money Boy and Mr. Raymoney to become that," she answered.

"But you're on the right path," he added.

At that moment, the bell rang and the students rushed to their classroom. Ms. Help was ready to start a new subject.

Victoria and Money Boy were barely paying attention, because they were busy with something else.

The girl handed over a piece of paper to her friend. It read:

> - Have you noticed Ms. Help doesn't wear a wedding ring?
> -

Money Boy had never thought about paying attention to that. However, he looked closer and noticed Victoria was right. He promptly wrote her back.

> - I don't care about those things. Why are you asking me that? What's wrong with not wearing a wedding ring?

Victoria was smart enough to answer:

> - There is nothing wrong with it, but it might be a solution for our problem-without-a-solution, from our friend, Spender!

Money Boy didn't understand what she was up to and answered her back.

> What does Ms. Help not wearing a wedding ring have to do with Spender's wish to have a little brother? Victoria, sometimes you confuse me. Do you know that?

She replied to him.

> Wake up! If the teacher dates Spender's father, maybe one day they could get married and have a baby! Got it?

Money Boy finally understood her idea and became excited about it.

> That's cool. I hadn't thought about that!

Victoria quickly wrote back to him.

> We can make up a plan.

Money Boy complimented her:

> You sure are a clever girl!

Victoria smiled when she read the note from Money Boy and placed it inside her pencil case. It was time to pay attention to Ms. Help.

During break, the three friends talked about Victoria's idea of bringing Ms. Help and Mr. Custódio, Spender's Father, together. They all agreed that it wouldn't be an easy task.

"Are you nuts!" Spender objected. "That doesn't have the slightest chance of working."

"Why do you say that? Your father surely misses having a girlfriend," argued Victoria.

"My father is a busy man. He doesn't think about having a girlfriend. He lives for his work."

"Well, I thought of something that might work out," Money Boy interrupted. "I call it a master plan."

"A master plan?" asked Victoria, scratching her head.

"Yes," answered Money Boy.

Spender, listening impatiently, asked, "What master plan?"

"Do you remember when we had that fight and they called your father into school to speak to the principal about us?" the boy began.

"I do. So what?" Spender asked.

"Well, for him and Ms. Help to meet he must be called in once again," continued Money Boy.

"Great! I already like it!" Victoria cheered.

"And what would make my father be called in again?" Spender asked.

"Here's the plan," Money Boy said. "We are having a language test this week, so I thought that if you turn in a blank test, with no answers on it, the teacher will be worried about you and will have to call your father in."

"Yeah. She will invite him to talk," Victoria said, smiling.

"A private talk?" Spender asked.

"That's right. Life will present you a challenge," Victoria repeated the lines she had learned from her mother, trying to convince her friend.

"Then I won't need to study for the exam!" Spender said, getting excited. "After all, to turn in a blank test takes no effort."

Money Boy - Friends helping friends

"Yeah, but afterwards you'll have to study twice as hard to get a better grade. Have you thought about that?" asked Victoria.

"Gee, that's right. I better not play around and start studying with the both of you right now," Spender agreed.

"So, welcome to the master plan then," Money Boy said.

"Friends helping friends!" Victoria said with enthusiasm.

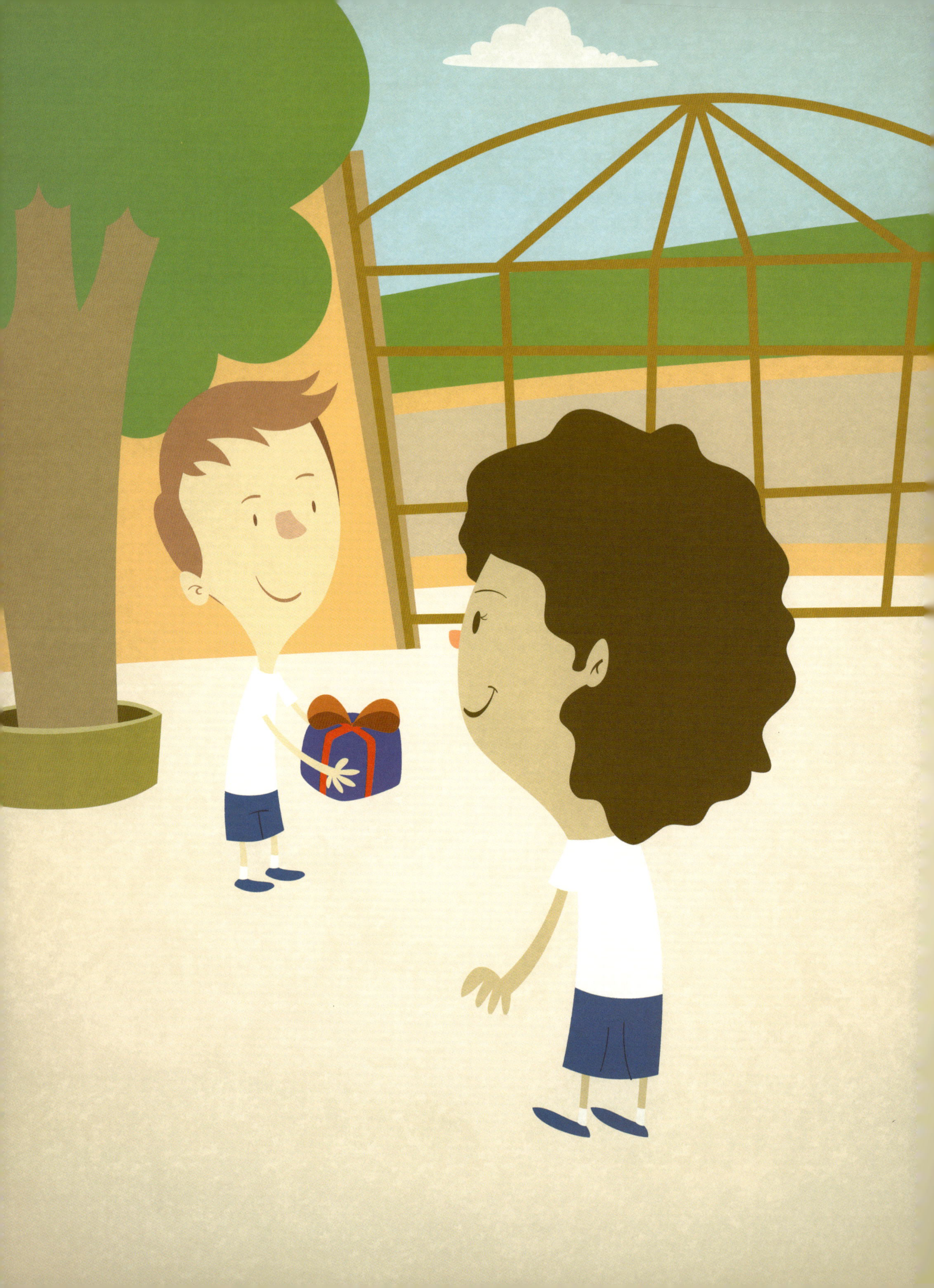

The magic formula

The following week, Victoria met Money Boy at the school gate holding a package under his arm. Restless and curious, the girl tried to find out what was inside that glossy wrapping paper.

"What's that you're holding?" the girl with the dimples asked.

"It's a present, of course!" answered the boy with a mysterious expression on his face.

"A present, huh. For whom?" Victoria asked.

"Do you want to guess?" Money Boy asked, blinking one eye.

"I don't have a clue. Tell me!" she said.

"It's for you, you silly girl." he answered giving her the package.

Money Boy's eyes were shining like bright lights while Victoria's dimples seemed more visible than usual around her smile.

The girl opened the package and was surprised with a cute, pink piggy bank.

Money Boy intended to teach Victoria the **DSOP Methodology** by giving his friend her very own piggy. He knew he should spread the Methodology to as many people as possible. And since Victoria was getting an allowance, it was about time she realized what to do with her money.

"Victoria, if you really want to become Money Girl, there are some things I need to teach you for that to happen," he said.

"What things?" she asked.

"If you learn how to save your allowance, soon you'll be able to make a dream come true. I'll explain better," Money Boy began. "I received a piggy bank once and started saving part of my allowance in it. I kept adding coins until it was full. Then I broke it and realized there was enough money for me to buy a dream of mine. One day I taught this same method to my dad. He also started to save and managed to have sufficient money to make his dreams come true."

"That's why you gave me this present?" asked Victoria.

"Yes! This way you are going to make your dreams come true and will have some money saved for emergencies, like the incident with your book. I broke my piggy to help you. If we save money, it will remain there to solve a future problem, if needed," Money Boy said.

"I get it. That's what you're always talking about, the **DSOP Methodology**, right?" the girl asked.

"That's right! Actually, it's a small part of it," he answered.

Money Boy told his friend about the methodology that Mr. Raymoney had taught him. He highlighted the little magic formula that had changed the life of his family.

The girl's eyes grew larger with curiosity. "Is it a magic formula?" she asked.

"Yes it is. It means Diagnosing, Dreaming, Budgeting, and Saving. That's why it's called DSOP," answered the boy, gesturing with his arms.

"Gee, it seems to be a treasure map," said Victoria. "How can we diagnose our own money? How can we do that?"

"It's simple!" said Money Boy. "Every day we must take notes of our expenses in a notebook. This way, by the end of the month, we can track where our money is going. For example, if I find out through my notes that I have spent half of my allowance on bubble gum, I can choose if I want to do the same in the following months, if it's really worth it, or if I want to buy something else with that amount."

"I see," answered the girl still a little confused.

"If I earn an allowance of $20 and spend $4 on bubble gum, I may satisfy my desire to chew gum at that moment. However, if I deposit the $4 in my piggy bank, I can achieve a much better thing in the future, like a new backpack for example."

"That is if you put $4 in every month, right?" she asked.

"Exactly! Diagnosing your allowance is to know the path your money is taking. When you write down your expenses, it is a lot easier to see what's best for you. Got it?" Money Boy asked.

"I get it. How about the dreaming part?" Victoria asked.

"That's the coolest part. We can close our eyes and wish for something we really want. Last year, I wanted a bike. I spent months filling up my piggy with coins to achieve that. On my birthday, I had already saved the amount needed to go to the bike store and purchase it. But instead, my father gave me the bike as a present and I was able to make another dream come true," the boy said.

"Cool! I want to dream and pursue my dreams just like you do," said Victoria.

"That's where the budgeting part starts, which is the third step of the methodology," explained Money Boy. "Most of our classmates receive an allowance and think they can spend everything throughout the month. According to the **DSOP Methodology**, the budget is done in a different way," he said.

"And how's that?" the girl asked.

"It's easy. You write down in a notebook the total amount of your allowance and subtract the amount you deposit in your piggy bank for your dream. Whatever is left you use to pay for your expenses, such as snacks and other daily expenses."

"My monthly allowance is $40. Should I put about $10 a month into my piggy bank?" the girl asked.

"The best plan is to actually know how much your dream is worth in order to estimate the monthly amount you should save. If you earn $40 and save $10 for your dream, you'll have $30 for your ordinary monthly expenses," explained Money Boy.

"I see, that budget is really kind of different," Victoria said. "Most people will first spend and if there's any money remaining, they'll save a small amount. In the DSOP budget, you first save for your dream and spend afterwards."

"That's right!" the boy said.

"I had never thought about it that way. I feel this is going to be very important for me from now on," the girl said.

"That's where the fourth step comes in, which is saving in a smart way. That is, filling up your piggy bank as fast as possible," said Money Boy. "I always put half my allowance in a piggy bank I have at home. When I earn some extra money, like on my birthday or when my grandma gives me some money, I deposit everything in my bank. I don't spend money on candy, stickers, keychains, and other things my friends love to buy."

"That's why they call you Money Boy," Victoria remarked. "You're really smart and have a way of thinking that's hard to see in other boys at school. Thanks for teaching me all that. I'll never forget it."

"No need to thank me," said Money Boy. "Just promise me that one day you'll buy three piggy banks like the one I'm giving you now. Give them away to people who you think are ready to learn about the **DSOP Methodology**. The more people we can help, the better."

Money Boy walked into his classroom, where Mr. Raymoney was writing the word "entrepreneurship" on the board.

"Today we'll be addressing some steps necessary for anyone to become a successful entrepreneur," he told the class. "It's important that you follow up very closely. So don't take notes just yet—simply listen."

Step 1: Enjoy what you do

"Any idea you decide to put into practice must be something that makes you happy. A successful job depends on your will to make that dream to come true. You have to be passionate about the entrepreneurial project you choose. The idea is to transform your project into a mission. That's why it's so important to enjoy what you do. "

Step 2: Planning and organizing

"To put a plan into practice, make a list of the necessary items for that idea to come true. If your project is to produce something, take notes of the material needed; find out where to purchase it at a cheaper price; figure out how long it takes your product to be ready; and determine where and to whom you are going to sell it. In addition, it's crucial to know exactly what the total expenses will be and how much your product will be worth."

Step 3: Knowing how to relate to people.

"To make things easier when putting a plan into practice, it is wise to be polite and to treat all your coworkers fairly. They are the people who will help you fulfill your mission. For example, the person who sells fruit to the Cool Stuff Company is a supplier, because he provides them with apples, grapes, and limes. The factory employees use the fruit to prepare the product. Children who buy the product at the school cafeteria are the customers. As a result, the supplier, the employees, and the customers, all work together with the Cool Stuff Company."

After the brief explanation, Mr. Raymoney answered questions and told the students there were still four more steps, but they would talk about them in the next class. He told them to review what they had learned and to do the exercise in their textbook.

On their way out, the three friends set up a study group meeting, where they would also talk about their master plan. They had a mission to fulfill and Mr. Raymoney's lessons might come in handy. Maybe those steps could also be kind of a magic formula to achieve what they were planning.

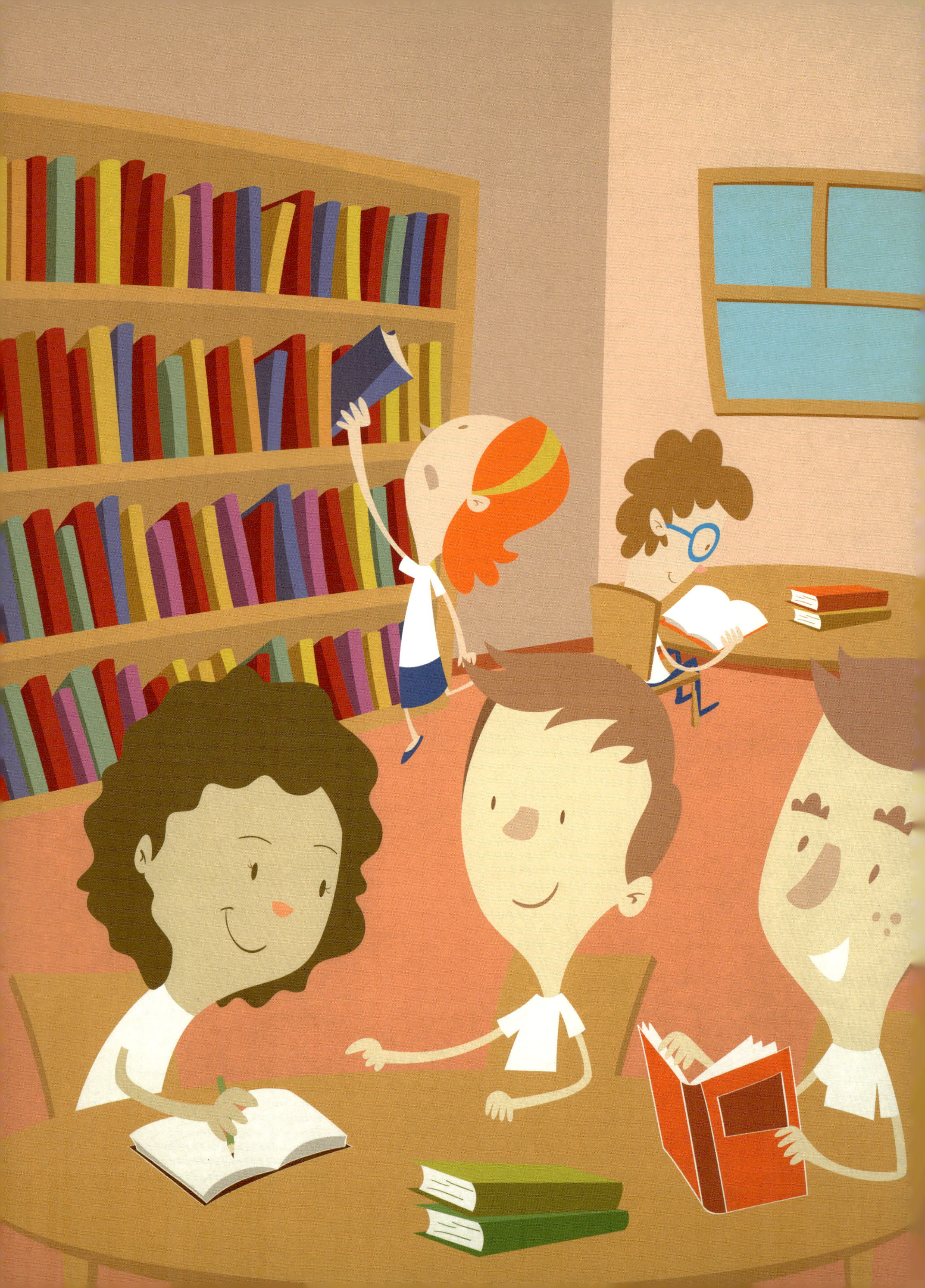

The secret mission

The following day, Money Boy, Spender, and Victoria gathered at the school library. They read over and reviewed the lessons regarding the first three steps of a successful entrepreneur. The three friends decided to use as an example, the idea of Victoria and her mother making notebooks.

"Well, the idea or plan is creating homemade notebooks, selling them, and earning money to make our dreams come true and to improve the life of our family," the girl said.

"Step 1 is enjoying what you do, and I believe your mother has taken that step already. Since she is a seamstress, I take it she loves working with fabrics, thread, needles, and stuff like that. Am I right?" Money Boy asked.

"Yes. My mom loves sewing! She gets so happy when she makes new clothes that she doesn't even notice the time passing by and keeps sewing until late at night," Victoria answered.

"How about Step 2? What does the notebook say, Spender?" Money Boy asked.

"It says here we should plan and set up. Oh, and there's also a list of things to do," replied Spender still sleepy. He wasn't used to being at school that early.

"Well that's a complicated list," the girl commented.

"We should also take notes of the places where your mother buys the things she uses," Money Boy added.

"I don't know where my mother buys thread, needle, glue, and string, but what I can say for sure is that the main thing we have at home, at no cost, is paper and leftover fabric from my parents' work," answered Victoria.

"The next item on the list," said Spender. "How long does it take for her to make the product?"

"Oh, my mother makes ten notebooks per week. I take them with me to school on Mondays," Victoria said.

"Where are the notebooks sold and to whom?" asked Money Boy.

"That's an easy one! We sell them at school to the students," Victoria said quickly, as if the words were on the tip of her tongue.

"And how much do you spend for making a notebook, and how much does it cost?" continued Spender.

"Ah, I don't know how much is spent, but we sell them for $10 each," Victoria replied.

"Now comes Step 3, which is relating to people," warned Money Boy.

"Ah, I don't think we do that," said the girl with the dimples.

"I think it's time we ask Mr. Raymoney for some advice, so your project with your mother may grow and work out right," advised Money Boy.

"Great idea! I will talk to him and I will also explain to my mother the steps we're learning," the girl said.

After some time, the three finished their homework and started talking about the master plan.

"Yesterday, during class, the teacher said in order to put a plan into practice, we've got to make a list with the most important items for our idea to come true. Do you remember that?" Victoria asked.

"Yes, that is part of Step 2, which is planning and organizing," answered Money Boy.

"That means we've got to set up our master plan," she said.

"Should we make a list?" asked Spender.

"I believe so. Look here," said the girl, writing down some items.

> Plan: Make Mr. Custódio meet Ms. Help and fall in love with her so Spender can have a little brother someday.
>
> List of important items:
>
> 1. Spender must submit a blank language test.
> 2. Ms. Help will invite Mr. Custódio for a talk.
> 3. They will meet and fall in love with each other.
> 4. Spender could invite Ms. Help over for dinner at his house.
> 5. Money Boy calls and gets Spender away from the table, leaving the two of them alone to get to know each other better.

Victoria stopped writing and began gathering her thoughts with the pen still held in her hand. Nothing more occurred to her to write.

"So, what else?" Spender asked anxiously.

"I don't know. I don't think we can go any further than that. If they start dating, it'll be great, but we can't force them," Victoria told him.

"That's true. We can only hope everything works out fine," said Money Boy.

The three friends put away their notes and went over to the cafeteria to eat lunch. Later on, they would have to be in class with Mrs. Constance. While eating, they talked about how funny it would be if the math teacher knew his lessons were not only good for teaching entrepreneurship, but also for helping them carry out their master plan.

They felt like superheroes in a secret mission and had Mr. Raymoney as an excellent partner, yet he didn't even know it.

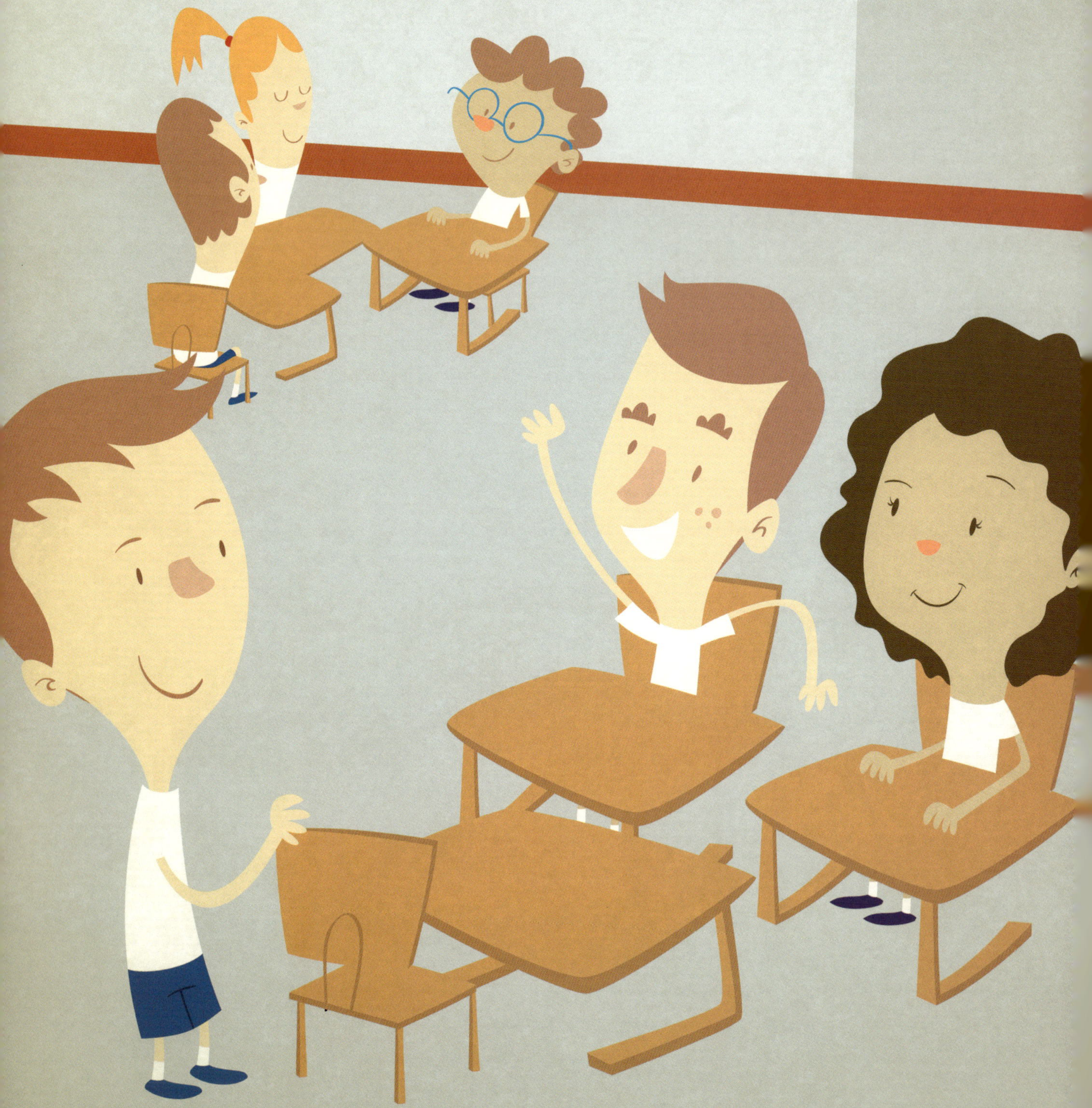

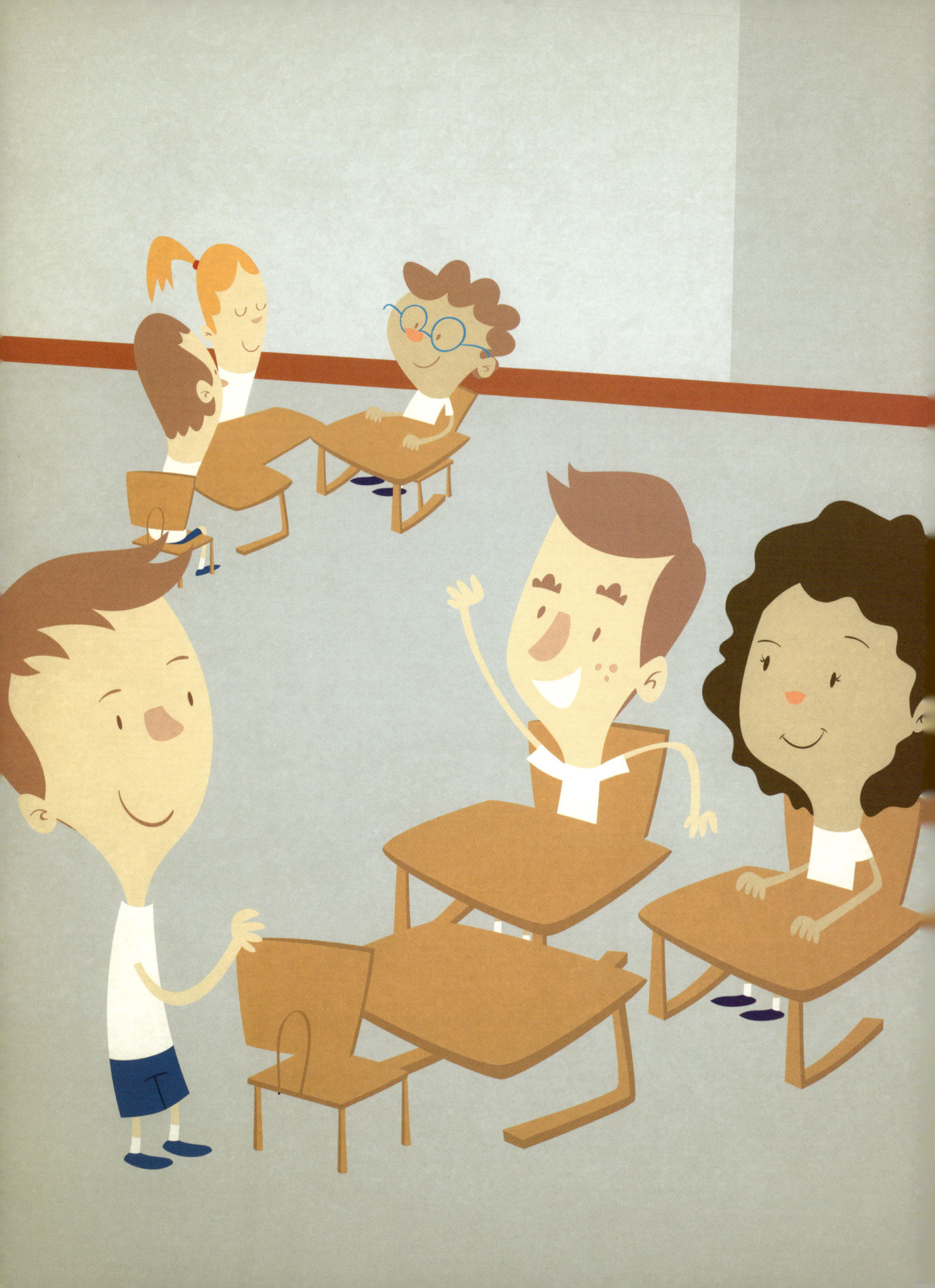

Word of honor

Another class of Mr. Raymoney had begun.

"Everyone, I want you to group up because from this class on we'll start developing a few projects," the teacher instructed. "I want you to choose an entrepreneurial idea and tell me how you intend to put it into practice."

"Do we have to start up a business? Are we going to work for real?" Spender asked.

"No. Kids can't work, but they can have ideas. You will set up a plan, of something that can yield money, just as my father started growing tomatoes and Mr. Custódio started up the soda factory. Do you remember that?" Mr. Raymoney asked.

The students nodded.

"You will figure out a product that can become a good business. Afterwards, you'll have to explain in an assignment how you can make that project real by using the seven steps we've learned in class," Mr. Raymoney said.

"But we only saw three steps so far!" said a boy in the back of the classroom.

"Well then, I'm going to teach the other steps today," answered the teacher.

Step 4: Spotting opportunities

"During the setup of a plan, you can bump into problems and opportunities. For example, when my father started selling tomatoes in the neighborhood, there was a time when people didn't want to eat them every day. It became a problem, because the tomato sales halted and we stopped earning money. Then my father started growing carrots and potatoes, too. That way the business kept growing and getting more customers. That's dodging the problems and spotting new opportunities."

Step 5: Being strong willed

"When you start working on an idea, you must be persistent in order for it to work out. There will be good and bad times; better and worse periods; but you can never give up. That word doesn't exist in the entrepreneurial world. You need perseverance, which is a lot of strength and faith to make your project succeed."

Step 6: Keeping your word

"When you set up a plan and work to make it become a real business, you have to stick to what you had in mind. For example, if my father promises the owner of the largest restaurant in town that he will be delivering 200 tomatoes on August 20, he has to keep his word. The restaurant owner is counting on that delivery of tomatoes to make his dishes and to serve them to his daily customers. Your word is like gold and it shows who you really are. If you don't keep your word, people won't make deals with you and won't trust you. In business, your word given is worth a million dollars."

Step 7: Aiming for profit.

"To be considered successful, a business has to be profitable. When a business pays its debts and there is still some money remaining, we call that amount profit. If my father's business earns $500 selling tomatoes and spends $380, there will be $120 left over. That amount is the monthly profit of the business. It's important that you become aware of this, because every entrepreneurial business needs to be profitable."

When Mr. Raymoney ended that last sentence, the bell rang announcing break time. Everyone ran off to the courtyard—some craving for a soccer ball, others more interested in buying things in the cafeteria.

Money Boy and Spender left for a table tennis match. Victoria, surrounded by girls, showed the new patterns of the notebooks made by her mother.

Back in the classroom, it was time to put the master plan into practice.

Ms. Help handed out the exams for the students and, half an hour later a courageous Spender stood up and left a blank sheet on the teacher's table. He placed it facedown, so she wouldn't immediately notice that he hadn't answered any of the questions.

The dye has been cast, strong will was at stake, and life wasn´t stopping! Spender had started the master plan and risked failing his exam.

Victoria seemed anxious and sent out good vibes, so everything would turn out fine. Money Boy's heart pumped hard, almost jumping out of his chest.

"That help among friends had to work out." he thought.

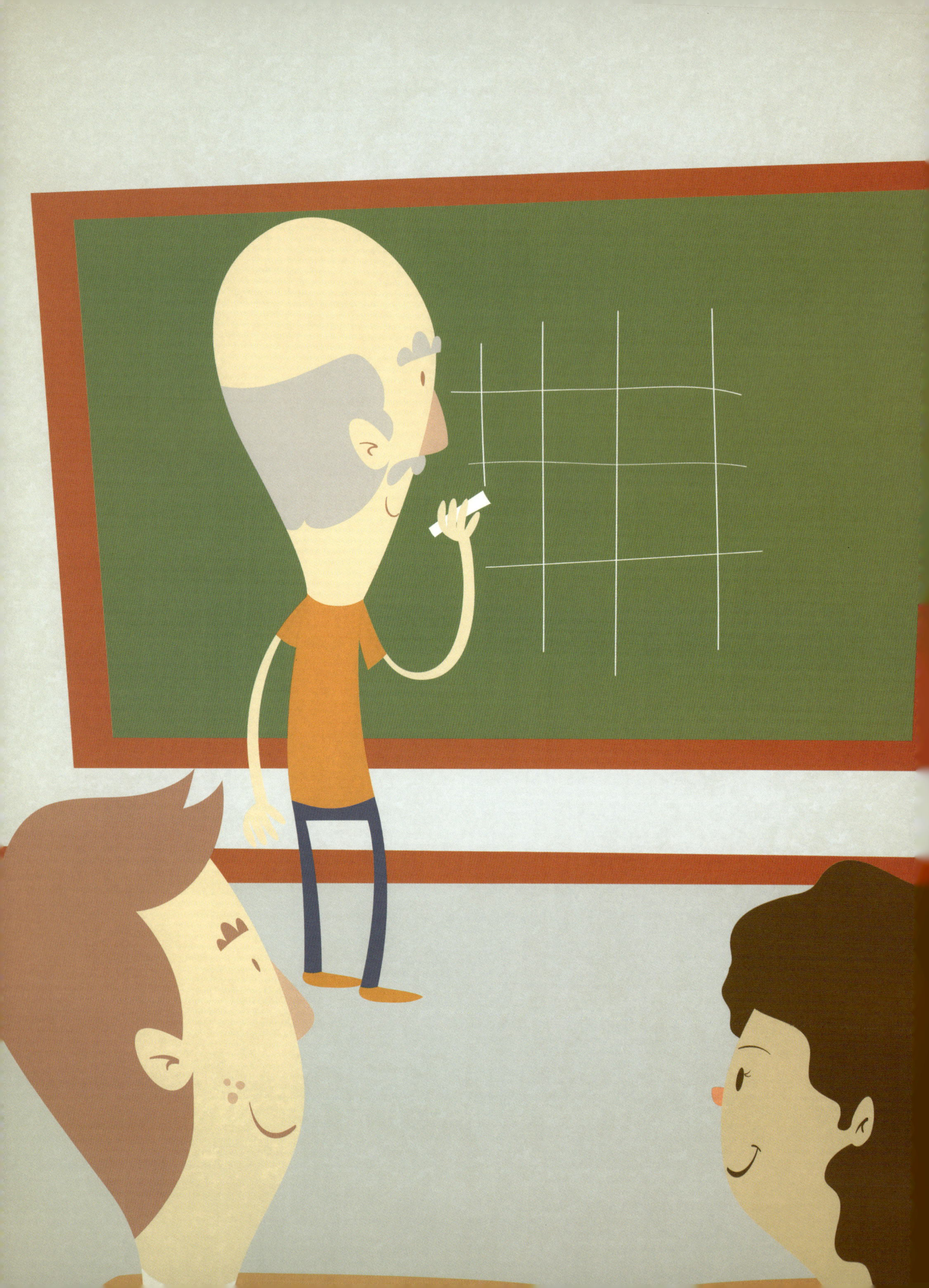

Magic mirror on the wall

The following week, Money Boy and Victoria entered the classroom. Spender was already there waiting, since Mr. Raymoney had asked the groups to get together and fill up a spreadsheet.

The task was simple. On the board, the teacher had written some information about his family's tomato business. He asked the students to fill in the blanks on the chart, considering each tomato box had sold for $1.

He wanted to demonstrate the mechanics of a cash flow, that is, the income and outcome of money. The first part of the "problem" was to figure out how much the business "earned" from the sales.

DATE	ITEMS	INCOME
AUGUST 1	500 tomato boxes sold	$500
AUGUST 10	600 tomato boxes sold	$600
AUGUST 20	900 tomato boxes sold	$900
AUGUST 25	500 tomato boxes sold	$500
AUGUST 29	100 tomato boxes sold	$100
GRAND TOTAL		$2,600

Furthermore, the teacher wrote on the board the business expenses and asked the students to calculate their monthly profit.

Date	ITEMS	INCOME	OUTCOME	RESULTS
August 1	500 tomato boxes sold	$500	$0	$500
August 10	600 tomato boxes sold	$600	$0	$1,100
August 16	Purchase: planting stuff	$0	$600	$500
August 20	900 tomato boxes sold	$900	$0	$1,400
August 25	500 tomato boxes sold	$500	$0	$1,900
August 28	Expense: stocking and deliveries	$0	$800	$1,100
August 29	100 tomato boxes sold	$100	$0	$1,200
August 30	Employees payroll	$0	$1,500	$-300
Grand total				$-300

The students were surprised after calculating and figuring out the final result, which showed that the outcome (expenses) was bigger than the income (sales).

Simply by looking at the first line, Victoria raised her hand with a question.

"Mr. Raymoney, what happens when the total adds up to a negative amount, when the business is spending more than its income?" she asked.

"In that case, the company will have losses instead of profits," said the teacher.

"And what happens when the company has losses?" the girl asked.

"The company runs out of money to pay its employees and to buy more material, among other things," answered Mr. Raymoney.

"Could you explain that better, please?" asked the girl, showing a genuine interest.

"When a business project accumulates losses, the company has to work twice as much to make up for the money it has lost," the teacher explained.

Victoria was thinking. It had been a day with too much information. Quickly, she got a piece a paper and outlined something that had been stuck in her head:

Date	Item	Earned	Spent	Left
January 5	Grandaddy's gift	$5.00	$0	$5.00
January 10	Aunt Anna's late Xmas gift	$10.00	$0	$15.00
January 15	2 golden magic rings	$0	$4.00	$11.00
January 18	2 colored beaded bracelets	$0	$3.00	$8.00
January 22	Bunnyfoot keyring	$0	$1.50	$6.50
January 25	Strawberry scented pencil	$0	$2.00	$4.50
January 28	Pair of doll shoes	$0	$5.00	$-.50

The more she wrote, the more stunned she became with what she realized. She had a worried expression over her face and the small dimples, that were sparkling a while ago, now had vanished away. The girl remembered the little bunny foot keychain she had purchased at a flea market a few months ago. She didn't even remember where she put it. Gradually, Victoria realized she was spending her money on things she didn't need to have.

When he saw the girl quietly drawing on her paper, Money Boy came closer to see what was keeping her so distracted. Victoria quickly closed the notebook and told him to mind his own business.

Actually, she was ashamed to show her friend how poorly she had managed her own money. Victoria wrote down only the month of January, when she was on vacation. She needed to track down the path her money had followed in the other months up to the present time.

Just by looking at the spreadsheet, the girl realized she wasn't being smart at all. If she really wanted to become Money Girl, she would have to resist the impulse of buying things that were not that important, such as bracelets, colored pens, lucky rings, and a whole lot of trinkets.

It was like that sheet of paper with all her expenses suddenly had changed into the mirror she had in her bedroom. For the first time, she realized that numbers show us who we truly are.

At that moment, she was a girl who spent more than she earned and she definitely wanted to change that.

When the class ended, the three friends met up at the school library to try to setup the notebook business for Mrs. Efficiency, which was their assignment for the end of the semester. The final meeting would be in a couple of days.

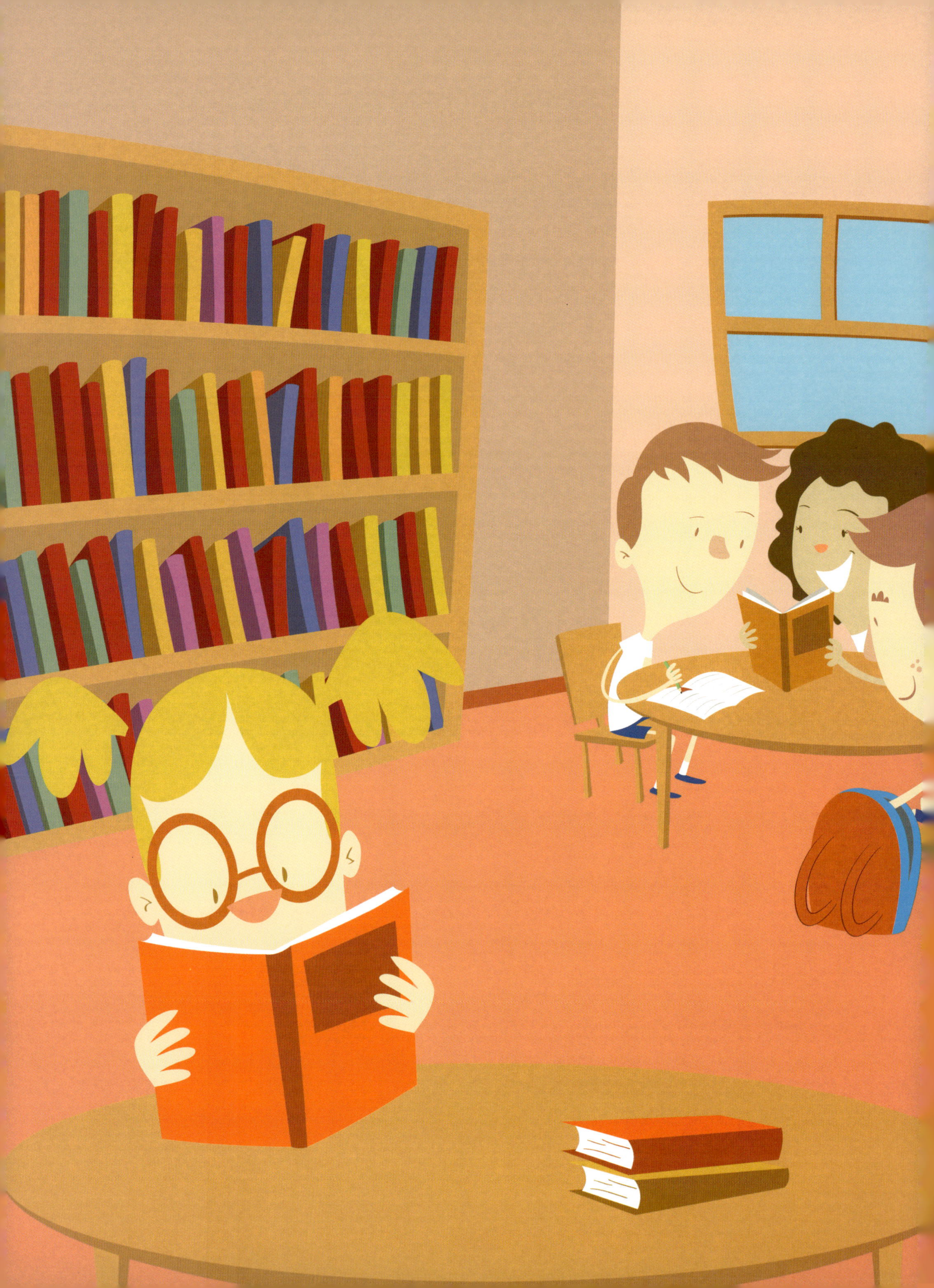

Giving up is for the weak

Several days later, Money Boy, Victoria, and Spender met at the library once more to work on their entrepreneurial project.

Notebooks and books open, they started by reviewing the tomato business spreadsheet they had filled out during class.

Spender took a sheet of paper out of his backpack and told his friends he had talked to his father the night before. Together, both of them filled up another spreadsheet, using Cool Stuff ice cream and soda factory as a model.

Money Boy and sweet Victoria looked curiously at their friend's notes, while he went through all the numbers that explained how the ice cream and soda factory worked.

Date	Item	Income	Outcome	Results
February 1	5,000 soda glasses sold	$10,000	$0	$10,000
February 5	10,000 fruit purchased	$0	$2,500	$7,500
February 10	5,000 ice cream scoops sold	$5,000	$0	$12,500
February 15	Employees payroll	$0	$8,000	$4,500

It was a simple spreadsheet, but one could easily see that in the end there was plenty of money left for Spender's father and his family to make their dreams come true.

While she was thinking about it, Victoria was feeling sad for her friend, because she knew that despite all of that money, he could not afford his biggest dream. A little brother wasn't on sale anywhere.

Only when her friends called her to fill up another spreadsheet did Victoria come out of those thoughts. This time they filled the information for her mother's handmade notebooks business.

When they finished, the three of them put away their school stuff and went to the cafeteria to have lunch. As they ate, Victoria told jokes and the buys laughed and had lots of fun with the girl with the dimples.

In the afternoon, they entered their classroom and Mr. Raymoney called them to present the first steps of their entrepreneurial project:

"Our group took notes on the money income and outcome of my mom's notebook business. We brought the March spreadsheet to show that things are going pretty good, because she's earning more than she's spending," Victoria reported.

The girl took a block of notes out of her pocket and told the class, using her own words, about the money path of Mrs. Efficiency's small business.

Date	Item	Income	Outcome	Results
March 10	40 notebooks sold	$400	$0	$400
March 12	Purchase of string, brush and glue	$0	$20	$380
March 15	Purchase of needle, thread and scissors	$0	$18	$362
March 25	10 notebooks sold	$100	$0	$462

Mr. Raymoney took the opportunity to remind the students that when a business is making more money than its expenses, it means it's being profitable.

"According to the group's spreadsheet there was a $462 earning," the teacher stated.

"Yes! By selling 50 notebooks, she managed to pay for the material and there's even a little extra," Money Boy announced.

"What should Victoria's mother do with that extra?" asked Mariana, the smartest girl in class.

"That's the point. That's an excellent question, Mariana. As we have seen in the seventh step of entrepreneurship, that extra is called profit," Mr. Raymoney said. "It shouldn't be spent, unless for something that will benefit the company. Mrs. Efficiency must take good care of that profit so it can grow bigger. But this is something we will learn next semester, when we speak about financial sustainability."

The bell rang and everybody walked to the courtyard and to gym class. The girl with the dimples wouldn't stop chatting about that profit thing they had just learned.

She realized the notebook sales proved to be profitable and that would help the so-called financial sustainability in her business.

On the other hand, she felt uncomfortable because, personally, she wasn't doing the same. She spent more than she earned, so her piggy bank remained almost empty.

All of sudden, Spender choked on his food when he saw his father crossing the schoolyard and entering the teacher's room. The master plan seemed to be working and the boy's heart was pumping fast and full of hope. He thought maybe some years from now he would have a chance to see his family growing with the coming of a little brother.

At the end of the arts class, Ms. Constance let the students out half an hour earlier, because they were finished with the classwork.

On his way home, Money Boy thought about how much fun it would be to teach his little brother to play soccer and ride a bike. Victoria thought about the notes she had taken. She made her diagnostic and found out she hadn't been treating her money the way she should. She decided to change her spending behavior and become a more balanced and conscientious girl. Now that became her greatest dream.

Meanwhile, Spender hoped his father wouldn't yell at him too much, and he trusted the crazy master plan to be successful.

Money Boy, Victoria and Spender all carried in their heart the hope that their wishes would come true and, as the fifth step in the entrepreneurship lesson said, a lot of perseverance.

They had learned from Mr. Raymoney's class that in life there are good and bad moments, but we can't give up, because that word doesn't even exist in the entrepreneurial world. It didn't exist in the world of heroes either.

Giving up is for the weak, the three of them thought while they headed home.

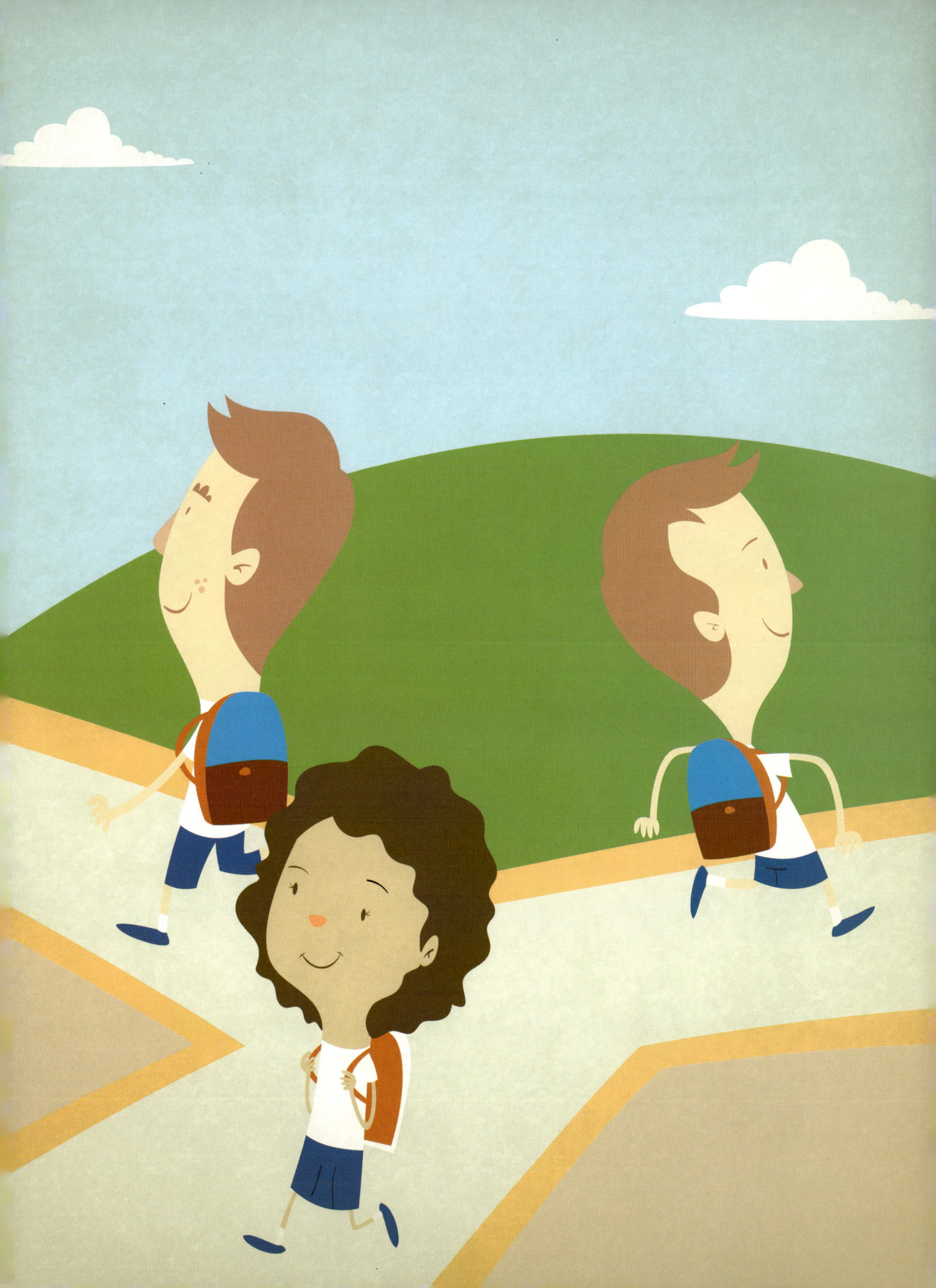

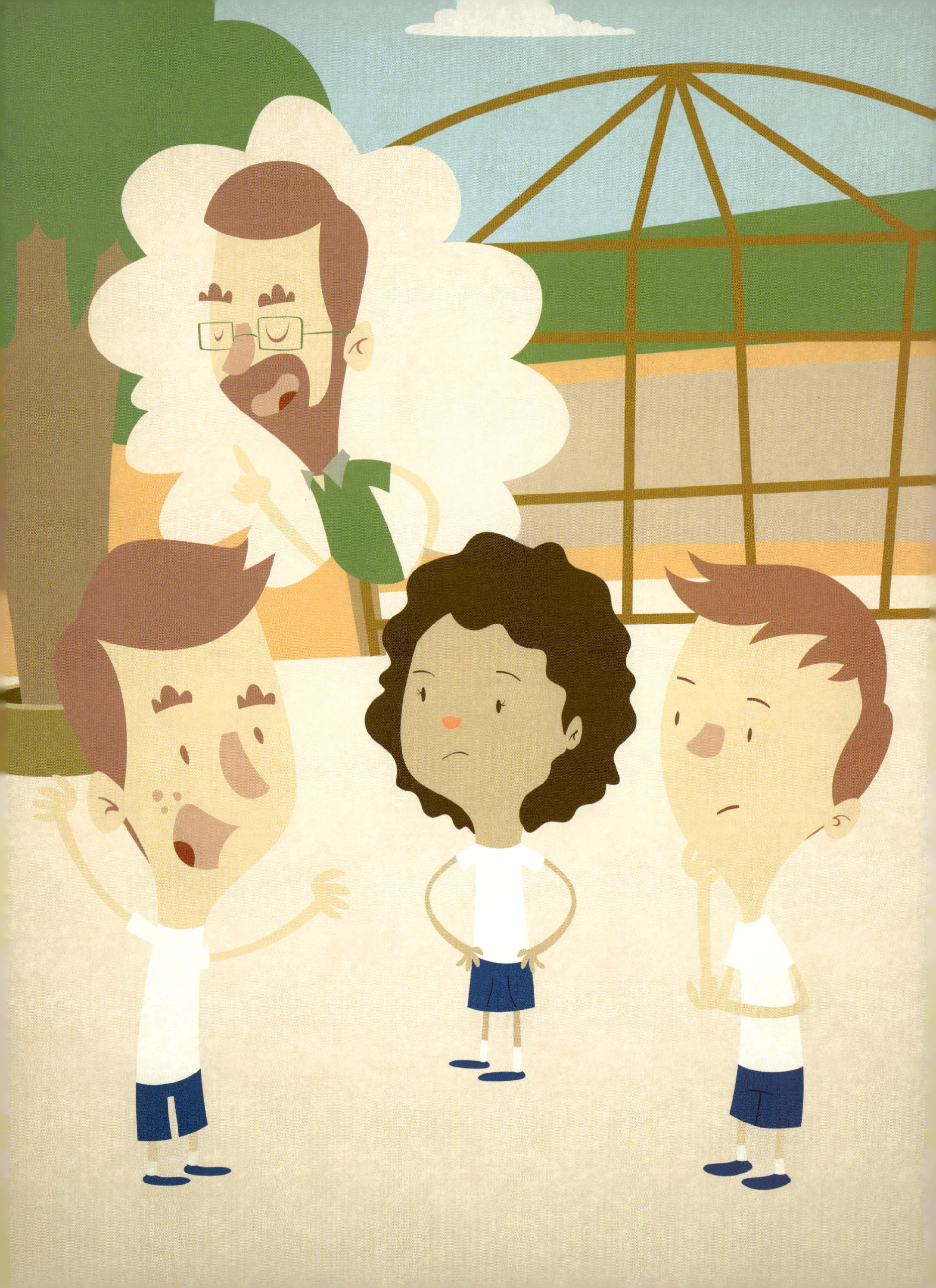

Roll call

Money Boy and Victoria waited anxiously in the schoolyard for Spender to arrive, because they wanted to know how the conversation went between Mr. Custódio and Ms. Help.

Spender approached his friends and finally satisfied their curiosity:

"It was better than I could have imagined," Spender said. "My dad was very angry when he first saw me, but eventually he calmed down. The more he yelled at me, the sadder I became in front of him, so I think he felt bad. When I had my chance to explain, I said the exam was complicated and I was having a tough time understanding that subject. In the end, I'll spend a month without playing my videogames and without watching TV as well, but you're not going to believe this," he said, creating suspense.

"What? Speak up!" Victoria shouted impatiently.

"My father hired Ms. Help to give me private classes three times a week. She will be coming over to my house often," the boy declared.

"Our master plan is a hit!" Victoria said loudly.

"Oh, boy, our master plan turned out better than we expected," added Money Boy.

"The bad thing about this is I'll have to study harder," Spender said.

The three of them laughed out loud. They were happy with the recent developments.

Everything was falling into place and their dreams were getting closer to each other. On that day, during class, Mr. Raymoney wrapped up the semester by taking a roll call. He wanted to be sure that the students had understood the seven steps of entrepreneurship.

"Gabriel, what is the first step of entrepreneurship?" the teacher asked.

"Enjoying what we do. That's step 1," answered the boy.

"Give me an example, please," asked Mr. Raymoney.

"A good example is my uncle Pablo. Since he was a little kid, he loved cars and now he owns an auto store."

"Very good Gabriel," the teacher praised him. "You just got some extra credit for your semester grade."

Moving forward, Mr. Raymoney pointed to Spender:

"Spender, please explain to the class what the step 2 of entrepreneurship is all about."

"It's the list step," stuttered the boy.

"What do you mean? the teacher asked.

"It's the rule that teaches us how to make a list of tasks to make our dream that is our business, come true," Spender said.

"Please give me an example of that," Mr. Raymoney said.

"Well, at Cool Stuff, which is my family's business, we have to make a list of how we sell our soda, how much we spend, and how much we make, things like that," explained the boy.

"Yes, that was a good example," the teacher agreed.

"Ah, I remembered. Planning and organizing are the best words to define the second step, teacher," the boy explained better.

Spender also got a better grade and Mr. Raymoney chose little Manuela to talk about the step 3 to the classmates.

"Knowing how to relate to people, teacher," answered the girl.

"Tell me a little more," asked Mr. Raymoney.

"We have to keep good relationships with people, because they can become our partners, buying our product or helping us with our business," the girl recalled.

"Very well, Manuela!" teacher congratulated her.

"Now I'm going to ask Money Boy to explain to the class about step 4 of Entrepreneurship," the teacher continued.

"Oh, that's an easy one. The fourth step is about creating opportunities and identifying problems. Spender's father, for example, started up his business making ice cream. Then he began selling sodas and invented other fruit-based flavors. All that helped to create new opportunities for his business," the boy answered.

"Very well," said Mr. Raymoney. "I see that you are all really engaged in the subject of entrepreneurship."

"Sure, we are engaged in many things, and your classes have been very important to our plans," added Money Boy, leaving the teacher very pleased.

"I like it when I see my students that excited. Do you have anything else to add to that?" the teacher asked.

"These days I've noticed that my mother also appears to be an entrepreneur. Every day she goes out to sell door-to-door cosmetics and she has many old and faithful customers. She buys beauty creams from the factory and re-sells them for a higher price. I believe she makes good money out of it," Money Boy told the class.

"That's great. You mother is also an entrepreneur for sure," Mr. Raymoney confirmed.

The teacher then asked Mariana, who was sitting in the first row, to talk about Step 5. "Willpower makes our business successful. We can never give up our wishes and must believe and persevere so our plan can work out right," answered the girl.

"Very well, Mariana. Good for you," approved the teacher.

Right before the bell rang, Saul, the tallest boy in class, also got a better grade for detailing Step 6 of entrepreneurship to the class:

"Giving your word, teacher. Sticking to the promised things, just the way it was agreed on, on the right date, at the right time," he concluded.

That moment, Victoria raised her hand to talk about the Step 7, her favorite.

"Profit comes when the first six steps are followed accordingly. It consists of what's left after we pay for our expenses," the girl explained.

"Excellent, Victoria!" the teacher said.

Seizing the opportunity, Victoria showed the teacher old notes of the expenses she had made in January and asked him to check the new spreadsheet with the expenses and the pathway of her allowance money.

Date	Item	Income	Outcome	Results
April 5	Mom's allowance	$40	$0	$40
April 6	Money put in piggybank	$0	$20	$20
April 12	Easter gift from auntie Simone	$20	$0	$40
April 18	Fairies deck of cards	$0	$10	$30
April 25	Movies	$0	$6	$24

At that point, Raymoney explained to the classroom that the money the girl put into her piggy bank couldn't be considered an expense, but rather an investment for achieving a dream.

Everyone clapped their hands, whistled, and cheered. Victoria blushed, but gave a discreet smile, showing her dimples. Her classmates were joking and said they now had a Money Boy and a Money Girl amongst them.

Mr. Raymoney ended the roll call and realized the students had learned the basis of entrepreneurship and they seemed to be enjoying those lessons.

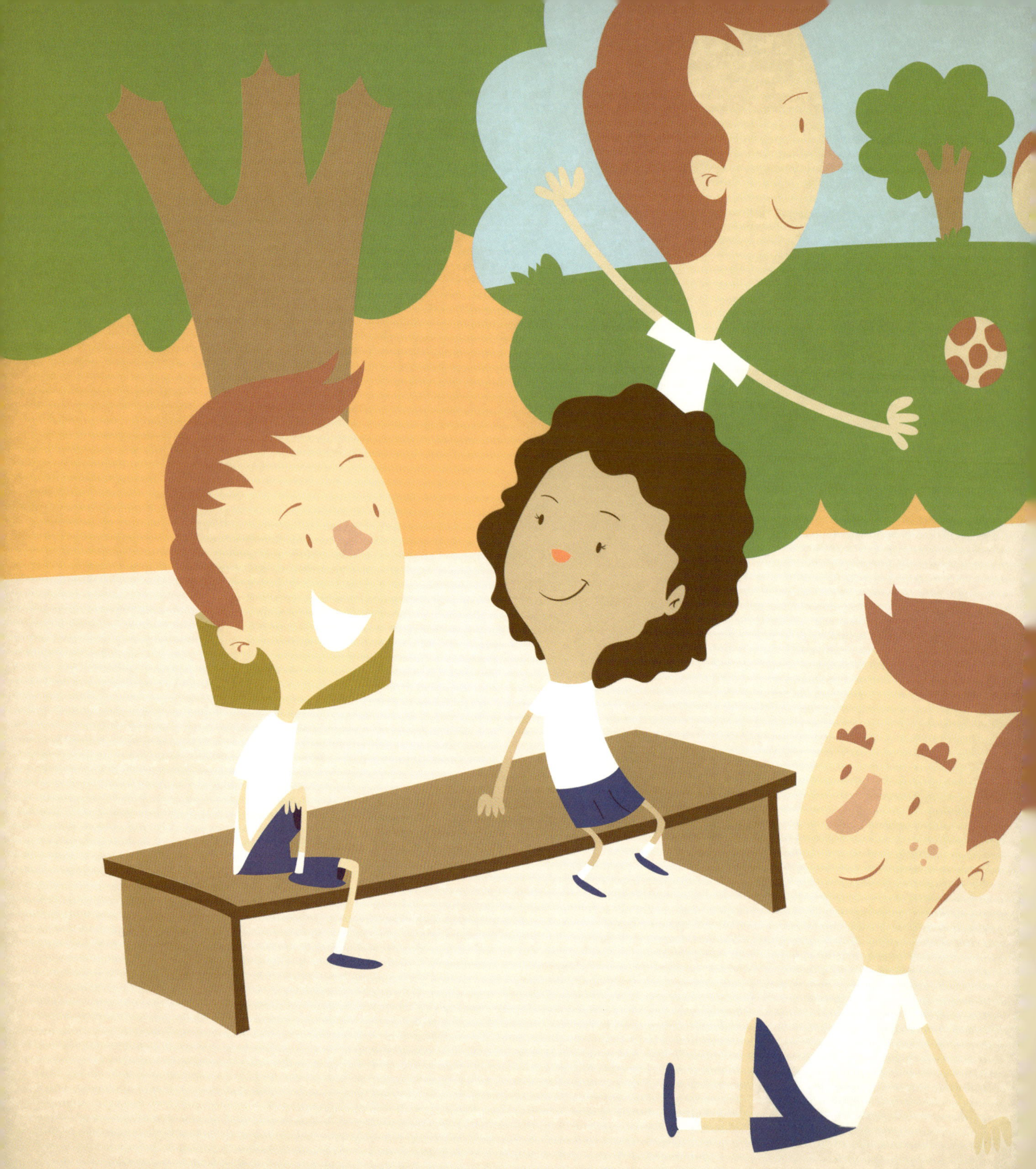

The best things in the world

The school semester would end soon and everything had worked out fine with the three friends. Victoria felt even more excited that her mother's notebook had become such a success. Spender also had reasons to celebrate, because Mr. Custódio and Ms. Help were dating steadily. The master plan had given him a few punishments and a low grade, but, on the other hand, it had opened up a way for him to have a younger brother in the future.

Money Boy became a little anxious though. His mother's belly grew enormous and the baby just hadn't shown up yet. He had begun karate lessons and hoped to teach his little brother some karate lessons as soon as possible. In addition, Money Boy took notes every day to keep a list of all the things he intended to show and explain to his brother as soon as he came into the world.

"Take it easy, Money Boy," said Victoria.

"I know, but it's just that I've waited for so long. I keep wondering what he will look like, which color his soccer shoes will be when we're up to play a match together. I've created a list of the 'best things in the world' that I want to enjoy with my little brother," he told his friend.

"A list of the 'best things in the world?' How wonderful!" said the girl with the dimples.

"Why don't we set up a master plan for this baby to be born soon?" asked Spender with a smile.

"That's an awful idea," answered Money Boy. "I'm anxious, but that's not a case for a master plan."

"I agree," Victoria said. "The master plan for you now is to be patient."

"Master plans are for unsolvable problems, just like yours, Spender," Money Boy said.

"That reminds me, I haven't told you what I did!" said Spender.

"What?" asked Victoria.

"My father, Ms. Help and I had dinner last night at my house. We talked and talked and I ended up telling them about our plan to get them together. And you know what's most surprising?" Spender asked.

"Speak up!" said Money Boy with an anxious tone of voice.

"They said they were suspicious and Ms. Help had noticed I already knew many of the subjects on the exam,"

"Wow! Really surprising! And why did you decide to tell them, Spender?"

"Ah, I don't know exactly, but since we're a happy family now, I don't think I have to hide anything from them," Spender replied.

The school principal walked over and interrupted the conversation to tell Money Boy that his father had called and said his mother was on her way to the hospital.

Money Boy's eyes lit up like two bright lights. Mrs. Constance, who was passing by, offered to take him to the hospital.

The two of them rushed and left Victoria and Spender behind.

"How cool is that? We're going to have another kid to take part in our future plans," remarked Spender.

"It's going to be great," Victoria said. "And years from now, we are going to have your brother as well."

At the end of the day, Money Girl came home and ran up to talk to her mirror. Many things were on her mind: diagnosing, dreaming, budgeting, saving, planning, organizing, keeping herself in good terms with people, being strong willed, keeping her word, identifying problems, creating new opportunities, achieving profit, and finding a place in the world.

"What will Money Boy have written on his list?" she asked, whispering softly to the mirror.

Victoria stood still and waited for an answer from the silent mirror. Then she wondered about the items she would list on a sheet of paper—the things she would find the best in the world.

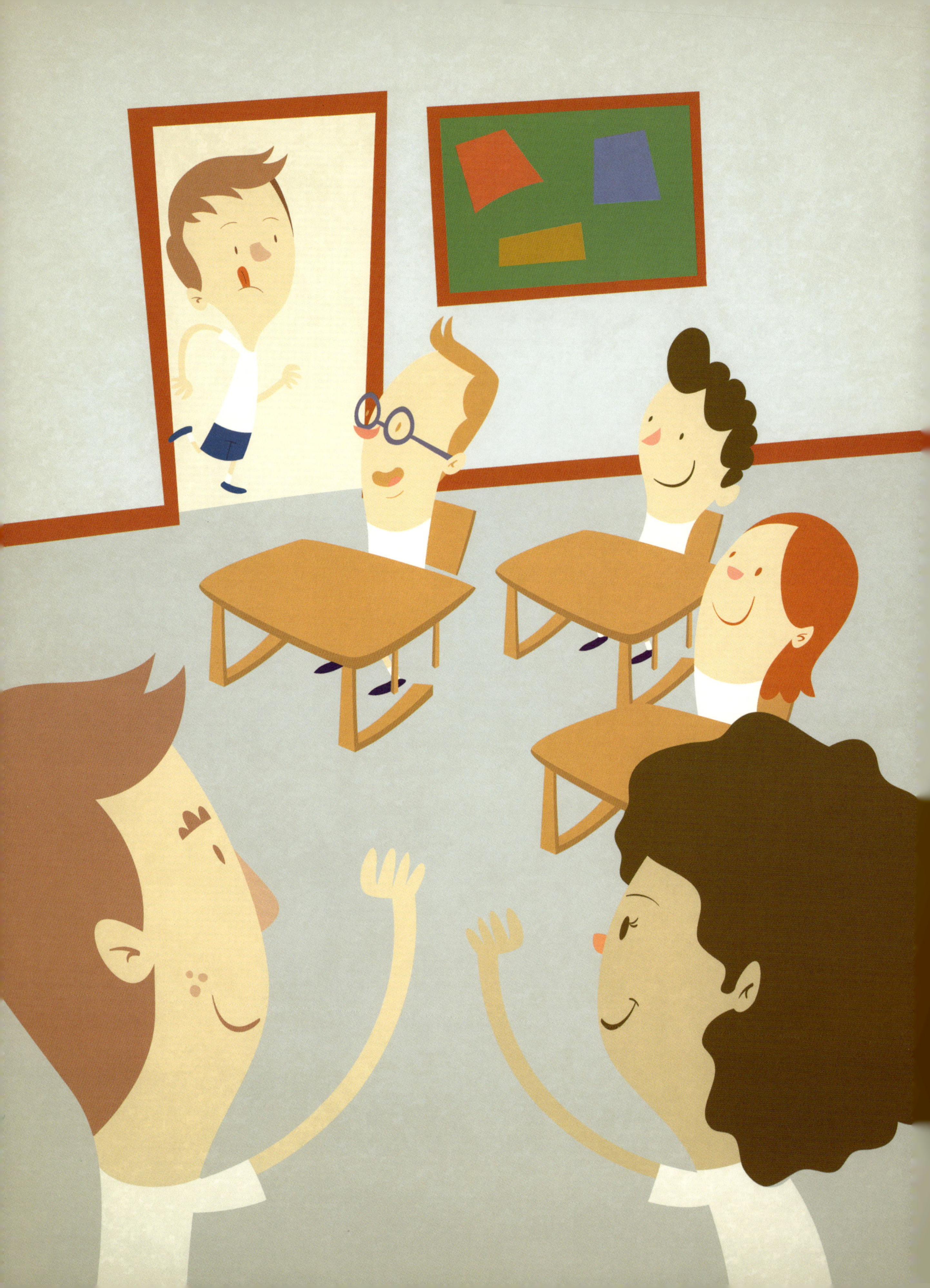

Tears of joy

Some days went by without Money Boy showing up for school. People knew his mother had given birth to a healthy baby and he had been away to welcome his brother and help his father at home.

However, the three friends needed to deliver their entrepreneurship assignment. The teacher was already in the class waiting for the rest of the students to arrive so he could begin the class.

Spender and Victoria looked at each other oddly. Although they had studied and prepared the whole semester, the team wouldn't be complete without Money Boy.

Everybody felt relieved when Money Boy arrived exactly when Mr. Raymoney called on the Recreate group. It was the name Mrs. Efficiency had given to her small business, and the three friends had borrowed it for their school assignment.

Victoria spoke about the first homemade notebook that she made for herself, after her own school materials were damaged at the beginning of the school year.

Spender explained how Mrs. Efficiency assembled the notebooks using cardboard, fabric, glue, thread, and needle.

Money Boy showed everyone Recreate's initial and most recent spreadsheets, that showed positive results by following the seven steps of entrepreneurship.

"Teacher, how can we be sure the Recreate business will keep on being successful in the future? In five or ten years from now, are there going to be students willing to buy notebooks?" asked one of the students.

"Gabriel, that's a good question. We will address that subject later on in our sustainability class, when we discuss how an entrepreneurship project can become sustainable and long lasting. It is indeed a great challenge, but it is a topic for next semester only," Mr. Raymoney said.

Money Boy's workgroup won a round of applause from the class and from Mr. Raymoney. The three friends smiled happily in front of their classmates and everything looked like a great party. Suddenly, they realized the teacher's eyes were full of tears.

The students started to calm down, the applauses faded away, and the room became completely silent as they waited for Mr. Raymoney to say something.

"Class, I want to say the greatest pride a teacher can have is seeing his students learning the lessons in class and using them in their lives. Last year, I taught Money Boy the **DSOP Methodology**, and I know he passed it on to many of you and to his own father. It managed to improve the quality of life for his whole family," Mr. Raymoney said.

"Today, I am moved by seeing that Victoria has also adopted the Methodology steps and is paying more attention to her money, taking notes of her expenses, and maintaining control of them. Mary and Jake are saving part of their allowances in a piggy bank to achieve their dreams. And, they're not the only ones. I know many of you are watching over your financial lives in different ways. That's why I want to thank all of you for keeping my dream alive. That is, teaching to those who are willing to learn."

The students came over to him and gave the teacher a big collective hug. Claps, cries of joy, and enthusiastic smiles spread all over the classroom.

Mr. Raymoney, excited and pleased, knew his teaching plan had become successful. He dreamed of a day when children throughout the world would have the opportunity to learn lessons that really made a positive difference in their daily lives.

Meanwhile, Money Boy, Money Girl, and brave Spender celebrated their achievement. They were certain they had gotten an A+ for a grade; however, it didn't seem that important anymore.

"Money Boy, if I was to make a list of the best things in the world, I think I would include Mr. Raymoney and the **DSOP Methodology** in it," said Victoria, among the noise of the celebration coming from her friends.

"And don't you think my list doesn't include them?" asked Money Boy.

They gazed at each other. She smiled, showing off her dimples.

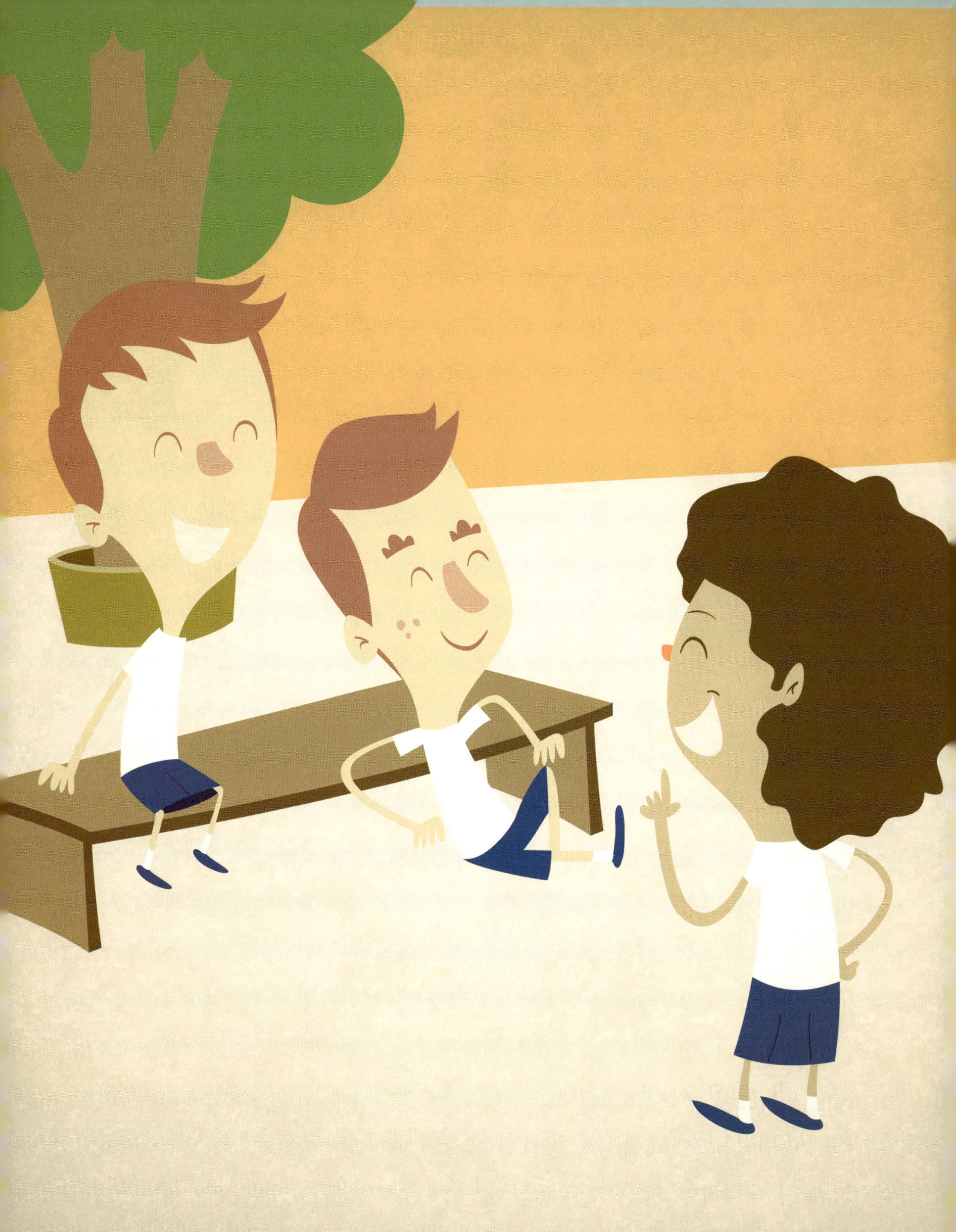

Special in a different way

The atmosphere in the schoolyard meant the end of the semester. However, both Money Boy and Spender were chewing gum and feeling slightly disappointed.

A breathless Victoria ran up to them, "Have you seen Ms. Help around?"

"No," Spender mumbled.

"What's up with you guys? You don't seem very happy," the girl said.

"Nothing much," he said.

"Yeah. Nothing much," Money Boy repeated.

"Come on, guys, tell me what's going on. Why are you so sad? We have many reasons to celebrate! What's up with you?" insisted the girl.

"Uh, my dad only has eyes for Ms. Help," Spender complained. "She is turning into a nagging stepmother for me. She keeps telling me to brush my teeth, comb my hair, and wash my hands before sitting at the table."

"I spent the whole year waiting for my mom to have a baby, because I wanted to teach him karate, soccer, skating and all sorts of things," Money Boy began. "And now what I have at home is a boring little girl, that probably is going to spend her entire life hooked on dolls, panty hose, ballet and pink clothes. Do you realize I'll have to take care of a girl with ponytails? That's boring!"

"Guys, you two are being so grumpy. Let's cheer up!" Victoria insisted.

"Spender, let me tell you one thing. The person who keeps telling us to brush our teeth and stuff like that is called a mother. Welcome to our world! You should be aware that combing hair and washing hands is very important for taking care of yourself, and that's the basics! By the way, weren't you used to doing that before?" the girl said, scolding him.

"As for you, Money Boy, you should review your opinions about girls because not every girl likes ponytails. You should rethink your list of 'best things in the world' so you can introduce your little sister to more interesting stuff other than soccer shoes or a kimono, because let's face it, that is so outdated." Victoria continued in an angry voice.

"So that's it! Go away, sadness! I want to see a large smile on the faces of you guys right now," the girl demanded.

Money Boy and Spender raised up their heads and looked mesmerized. There was a moment of silence and then the three of them broke out laughing.

"Victoria, you sure are a very special girl. I hope my little sister is like that when she grows up," Money Boy remarked.

"Am I special even if I don't play soccer or fight karate?" the girl asked.

"Yes! You know how to be special in a different way. If I was to do my list of 'best things in the world,' I'd put your name on it," Money Boy replied.

"And don't you think my list doesn't include your name?" she asked.

At that moment, Ms. Help crossed the other side of the courtyard and Victoria ran off to meet her. The girl with the dimples had a very important thing to deliver to her teacher. She had written a composition. Ms. Help put it inside her purse and read it when she arrived at home. Her eyes followed the sentences the student had written and many thoughts went through her mind. She was happy to realize that girl sure was a victorious one.

Dear teacher,

At the beginning of the school year, I still didn't know who I was and wrote you a composition with only a few sentences. Today I'm delivering you this new composition, because many things have happened during the semester. Now I can tell you that I'm a girl with lots of ideas in my head, who likes to face the challenges of life and who has the best friends in the world.

I have learned so many things, that I barely understand how it all can fit into my head. I've found out that dreams are twofold: those we can buy (a bike, a book, a trip) and those we have to conquer (friends, family, smiles, group hug, tears of joy, sincere compliments.)

After I understood that, life became much easier. I believe dreams come true when we strive for them to come true, and I believe giving up is for the weak. My father always tells me I have to find my place in the world, and that's what I do every day at school and with my mom's business.

My best friend, Ray, has taught me a magical formula that has helped me to take better care of my money. That formula is called DSOP, which stands for: diagnosing, dreaming, budgeting and saving. By using this formula, I became better known as Money Girl.

Sometimes I talk to my mirror and it shows me who I am. I am happy with what I see, and I can say three paragraphs are too short for me to write all the things I'd like to say about myself.

Author
Reinaldo Domingos

www.reinaldodomingos.com.br

Reinaldo Domingos is a master degree, professor, educator, and financial therapist. Author of the books: Financial Therapy; Allowance is not just about money; Get rid of debts; I deserve to have money; Money Boy—family dreams; Money Boy—goes to school; Money Boy—friends helping friends; Money Boy—in a sustainable world; Money Boy—little citizen; Money Boy—time for changes; The Boy and the Money; The Boy, the Money, and the Three Piggy Banks; The Boy, the Money, and the Anthopper; Being wealthy is not a secret; and the series Wealth is not a secret.

In 2009 he created Brazil's first textbook series of financial education aimed at grammar school, already in use by several schools in the country, both private and public. In 2012 he was a pioneer in creating the first financial education program for young apprentices. In 2013 that program also included young adults. In 2014 he created the first financial education course for entrepreneurs, followed by financial education as a university extension course.

Domingos graduated in Accounting and System Analysis. He is the founder of Confirp Accounting and Consulting and was the governor of Rotary International District 4610 (2009-2010). Currently, he is the CEO of DSOP Financial Education and DSOP Publishing. He is the mentor, founder and president of Abef (Brazilian Association of Financial Educators). He is also the creator of Brazil's first postgraduate course in Financial Education and Coaching and mentor of the **DSOP Methodology**.